BRITISH

Language & Culture

Acknowledgments
Associate Publisher Mina Patria
Managing Editors Bruce Evans, Martine Power
Editors Janet Austin, Kate Mathews
Managing Layout Designer Chris Girdler
Layout Designer Carol Jackson
Production Support Larissa Frost, Chris Love
Product Development Janine Eberle, Laura Jane, David Kemp, Micha[illegible] Ruff, Laura Stansfeld
Language Writers Dr Elizabeth Bartsch-Parker, Stephen Burgen, Richard Crowe, David Else, Dr Roibeard O Maolalaigh, Dominic Watt

Thanks
Sasha Baskett, Kylie McLaughlin, Trent Paton, Piers Pickard, Kirsten Rawlings

Published by Lonely Planet Publications Pty Ltd
ABN 36 005 607 983
3rd Edition – March 2013
ISBN 978 1 74104 826 1

Cover Image Cover montage by Andy Lewis. Cover photographs: abzee, altugphotography, Brian A Jackson, Duncan Walker, kertlis, Life on White, Lillis Photography, PeskeyMonkey, Sashkinw, Simon Bradfield/iStockphoto©

Printed in China 10 9 8 7 6 5 4 3 2 1

Contact lonelyplanet.com/contact

NORWEGIAN SEA
Unst
Yell
Fetlar
SHETLAND ISLANDS
Maintand
Foula
Fair Isle
Westray
Rousay
Sanday
Stronsay
Mainland
ORKNEY ISLANDS
Hoy
South Ronaldsay
NORTH SEA
Duncansby Head
Lewis
St Kilda
Harris
The Minch
North Uist
Little Minch
Benbecula
South Uist
Skye
Moray Firth
Loch Ness
Rum
Barra
Eigg
Sea of the Hebrides
Grampians
Aberdeen
Coll
Tiree
SCOTLAND
Mull
Dundee
Colonsay
Loch Lomond
Stirling
Firth of Forth
ATLANTIC OCEAN
Jura
Islay
Bute
Edinburgh
Glasgow
Arran
Southern Uplands
Kintyre
North Channel
NORTHERN IRELAND
Belfast
Machars
Carlisle
Solway Firth
Newcastle-upon-Tyne
Pennines
Isle of Man
GREAT BRITAIN
York
Leeds
IRISH SEA
NORTH SEA
Liverpool
Manchester
DUBLIN
Anglesey
Sheffield
ENGLAND
REPUBLIC OF IRELAND
Llyn Peninsula
Cambrian Mountains
Nottingham
The Wash
Wolverhampton
Leicester
Cardigan Bay
Coventry
Birmingham
St George's Channel
Cambridge
Ipswich
Cotswolds
Luton
WALES
Chelmsford
Swansea
Newport
Oxford
LONDON
Southend-on-Sea
Cardiff
Bristol
Reading
Bristol Channel
Canterbury
Lundy
Stonehenge
Winchester
Maidstone
Strait of Dover
Southampton
Brighton
Hastings
Exeter
Bournemouth
Portsmouth
Eastbourne
Isle of Wight
Lyme Bay
Plymouth
English Channel
Land's End
Isles of Scilly
Golfe de Saint Malo
FRANC
0 100 km
0 50 miles
Guernsey
Jersey

A SHORT HISTORY OF BRITISH

CLASSIC PHRASE:

'WASSSAMATTER WIV YER?'

The way they say 'What is wrong with you?' in the area around London

TRY THIS ONE:

SICK AS A PARROT

For times when 'I'm upset' just isn't emphatic enough

USE WITH CAUTION:

ENGLAND

Only use this term if you're referring solely to England; if you're also discussing Scotland or Wales, use Britain

MISUNDERSTANDINGS:

AIN'T NEVER DUN NUFFING

Not quite what the double negative infers, this Estuary English phrase means 'I haven't done anything wrong'

A SHORT HISTORY OF BRITISH

English is one of the most widely spoken languages on earth, and the closest thing we have to a global common tongue. It's the international language of science, business, aviation, technology and the internet - not to mention much of the international sporting circuit. It's the language of global cinema, and if you want to make it big in popular music, you generally sing in English - wherever you come from.

Originally derived from the dialects of obscure northern European tribes, English became the language of Britain around the middle of the first millennium AD, and as recently as the end of the 18th century the majority of English speakers still lived in England.

Today, however, English is the first language of around 400 million people globally, and the second language of perhaps 400 million more. It's the national language, official language or common language in more than 60 countries. In many parts of the world, English is the preferred second language - for example, it's the second language of choice of European school students, by a large margin.

"GOBSMACKED
— SURPRISED"

As English was exported across the world this once minor language developed into many different forms, so that the English spoken in America is different from that spoken in Australia, the English spoken in Ireland is different from that spoken in India – and they're all different from the mother tongue that spawned them.

This book is about British English – the English spoken by around 57 million people on the island of Britain. This may be the birthplace of English, but the language here certainly isn't static. The British take great pleasure in using the English language fully and inventively, and it continues to evolve and be exploited – sometimes with amusing results. For example, British politicians don't lie, they **dissemble**; kids aren't simply surprised, they're **gobsmacked**; football fans suffering a defeat aren't just sad, they're **as sick as a parrot**.

On it goes – British English is a tirelessly inventive language, borrowing without shame, outrageously playful, always seeking simplicity and yet revelling in complexity. We hope this book helps you enjoy the language as much as we do.

English roots & offshoots

Britain may be a small island on the edge of Europe, but its history has been far from insular. Over the millennia, waves of invaders and incomers arrived, settled and made their mark – and were (eventually) absorbed.

The same thing happened to the English language. In the 15 centuries of its existence, English has been notable for its openness to other languages, and its readiness to adopt, absorb or adapt foreign words. Take, for example, the various ways of describing the coming together of two or more people. It could be a **rendezvous** or a **reunion** (both borrowed from French); a **gathering** or **meeting** (both originally Old English); an **assignation** or **encounter** or **rally** or **tryst** (Old French). Together, they allow the speaker a remarkable degree of precision about the kind of 'meeting'.

A NOT SO UNITED KINGDOM

This book is about British English. The state of **Great Britain** is made up of three separate countries – England, Wales and Scotland. England is the dominant country, but the peoples of Scotland and Wales have kept a strong sense of national identity (perhaps precisely because of English dominance).

It's important to remember that the terms **Great Britain** and **England** refer to different political entities; they're not interchangeable, and to say England when you mean Britain will almost certainly put the backs up of any Scottish or Welsh people present. Scotland has a separate parliament and church, plus its own systems of law, banking and education; while Wales has its own National Assembly.

Just for the record, the **United Kingdom** (**UK**) consists of Great Britain, Northern Ireland and some semi-autonomous islands such as the Isle of Man. The island of Ireland consists of Northern Ireland and the Republic of Ireland (also called **Éire**). And for you scholars out there, **the British Isles** is a geographical term for the whole group of islands that make up the UK and the Republic of Ireland. The more politically correct term is **Britain and Ireland**.

For another example, just look at the nautical lexicon. Dutch has contributed **cruise**, **deck**, **freebooter** and **yacht**. The words **armada** and **galleon** are borrowed from Spanish, **buccaneer** and **frigate** come from French, **capsize** comes from Catalan, **kayak** from Inuit languages and **catamaran** from Tamil.

Before we go on to look at this fondness for borrowing in more detail, however, let's go back to the very beginnings of English.

Invaders

The withdrawal of the last Roman troops from Britain in AD 410 heralded another invasion, this one by the Angles and Saxons – Teutonic tribes from northern Europe, often lumped together by historians as Anglo-Saxons. They moved fast, and quickly absorbed or drove out most of the Romano-British inhabitants, introducing their own culture and language so thoroughly that by the late 6th century the country now called England was predominantly Anglo-Saxon.

The language of the Anglo-Saxons was the earliest form of English, and is now known as Old English. Linguists estimate that out of English's vast vocabulary only around 4300 words are derived from Old English, but these words are so basic – for example **at, child, drink, for, go, God, live, love, man, to** and **woman** – that they make up the bulk of everyday speech.

In fact, nearly all of the 100 most commonly used words in modern English are of Anglo-Saxon origin.

Take something fundamental like a **door**. Not only the term door, but also most of the associated words are Old or Middle English – **ajar, close, frame, handle, hinge, key, knob, lock, open, panel** and **sill**. Only a few terms are borrowed from other languages – **jamb** (from French) and **architrave** (Italian), for example.

> "DISSEMBLE
> — BEING ECONOMICAL WITH THE TRUTH; IE LYING"

A CUTE ANGLE

Of the missionaries sent to Britain in the 6th century, one holy pioneer was St Augustine, who successfully converted Angles in the area now covered by the modern county of Kent. Some good-looking specimens were sent to Rome as proof of Augustine's progress – giving rise to Pope Gregory's famous quip, *'Non Angli sed angeli'* ('not Angles, more like angels').

Missionary men

The Angles and Saxons were pagans, and their invasion forced the Christian religion of the Romano-British people to the edges of the British Isles – to Wales, Scotland and Ireland. The pope of the time, Gregory I, decided this was a poor show, and in AD 597 sent missionaries to Britain. This also had the effect of introducing words of Latin (the language of the Christian Church) into English. **Angel**, **candle** and **disciple** were all adopted during this period.

The victorious Vikings

The missionaries weren't the only early arrivals to the new Anglo-Saxon Britain. By around the 7th century, the Vikings (a catch-all term for the Norse or Nordic peoples from Scandinavia) had started to loom on the horizon.

School history books give the impression that Vikings turned up, raped, pillaged, killed, then left. While there's some truth in that, many Vikings settled in Britain for good.

There were two main waves of Viking invaders. The first came from the area now called Norway, and they attacked northern Scotland and the parts of northern England that are now Cumbria and Lancashire. By around AD 850 a second wave, from Denmark, had conquered and occupied east and northeast England, making the city of Yorvik (now called York) their capital.

From their northern territories, the Vikings then spread across central England until they were confronted by Anglo-Saxon armies coming from the south, led by the new king of Wessex, Alfred the Great. The battles which followed were seminal in the foundation of the nation-state of England, and although things didn't all go Alfred's way, by 886 he had managed to push the Vikings back to the north.

The Vikings' linguistic legacy is still evident in parts of Scotland and northern England in the place names and local dialects. Examples include places ending in:

- **-by** (from the Norse for 'farm', 'homestead' or 'settlement'), such as Grimsby or Derby
- **-thorp** (another word for 'settlement' or 'village'), as in Althorp or Scunthorpe
- **-thwaite** (a cleared piece of land), as in Braithwaite or Longthwaite
- **-toft** (an area of land), as in Lowestoft

Family names ending in **-son** (meaning, of course, 'son of') are also a Viking legacy.

In addition to names, the Vikings brought many everyday terms such as **dregs**, **egg**, **husband**, **knife**, **law**, **root**, **sly**, **take** and **window**.

English also adopted the Norse pronouns **they**, **them** and **their**. Old English already had the word **home** (with the same meaning it has today), but took on the Nordic word **house** as well – an early indicator of the preference for two or more words with the same broad meaning when the new word allows a different nuance to be expressed.

> “DREGS, EGG, KNIFE
>
> – VIKING TERMS”

In total, around 1000 words of modern English have Nordic origins, and the further north you go in Britain and Ireland, the more words of Norse origin survive. In the Shetland Islands, north of Scotland, as many as 1500 words of Old Norse remain in use.

Big wig William

Life remained unsettled for a few more centuries in England, as the royal pendulum swung between Anglo-Saxon and Danish-Viking monarchs. When King Edward the Confessor died, the crown passed to Harold, his brother-in-law. That should've settled things, but Edward had a cousin in Normandy (in today's France) called William, who thought he should have succeeded to the throne of England.

> "SICK AS A PARROT
> – UPSET"

The end result was the Battle of Hastings in 1066, the most memorable of dates for anyone who's studied British history. William sailed from France with an army of Norman soldiers, the Saxons were defeated, and Harold was killed – according to tradition by an arrow in the eye, the version of events recorded on the famous Bayeux Tapestry. William became king of England, earning himself the prestigious title 'William the Conqueror'.

The arrival of William the Conqueror was a milestone event, as it marked the end of Britain's linguistic and cultural ties to the Nordic countries (only in Orkney and Shetland did the Viking presence continue until the 15th century). Mainland Britain's focus shifted to France, western Europe and the Mediterranean, with massive linguistic and cultural implications. In addition, the Norman landing capped an era of armed invasion. Britain has not been seriously invaded by a foreign power in the 900-odd years since 1066.

In the years after the Norman invasion, the French-speaking Norman rulers and most of their English-speaking Saxon subjects kept to themselves. As with the Vikings, the invasion didn't eradicate the English language, although it had a huge effect on it. For around three centuries French was the official language, and English was virtually ignored by the educated elite of the church and state. As a result, as many as 10,000 words in the modern English language are derived from Norman French.

Most linguists believe that it was probably during this period, when English was left in the hands of the common people, that the process of simplifying it and stripping down its grammar began to accelerate.

Obvious examples of French borrowings are the terms of law and government, such as **adultery**, **court**, **justice**, **marriage**, **parliament**, **sovereign** and **tyrant**.

In later centuries, perhaps thanks to the **feudal system** (see the box on p16), English helped itself to the rich store of French words devised to express class distinctions, among them

FRIDAY ON MY MIND

Interestingly, the Vikings had the same gods as the Anglo-Saxons, so the days of the week were unaffected by the invasions. They were named after the sun and moon (**Sunday** and **Monday**), the Anglo-Saxon gods Tiw, Woden, Thunor and Frige (**Tuesday**, **Wednesday**, **Thursday**, **Friday**), and the Roman god Saturn (**Saturday**). The names of the months in English, by contrast, generally have Latin roots.

arriviste, **bourgeois**, **chauffeur**, **chauvinism**, **elite**, **faux pas**, **limousine**, **nouveau riche** and **parvenu**. The word **snobbery** itself is English, of course.

> "ARRIVISTE, ELITE, CHIC, PANACHE
> — FRENCH TERMS"

Even in modern times, no one has ever accused the English of being **chic**, and they've had to ransack French **bon mots** in order to acquire some **élan** and **panache**.

Pick & mix

The English language has kept on borrowing from anywhere and everywhere. Centuries of sea-borne trade, crusades and, later, the British Empire ensured that the British travelled around the world, both exporting their language and importing foreign words into it as they went. Without picking and mixing foreign words into the language, the British wouldn't now be sitting in their **pyjamas** (Urdu), living in **bungalows** (Hindi) or smoking **hashish** (Arabic).

There are thousands more words, borrowed over the centuries and now firmly part of mainstream English, like:

anorak (Inuit)
intelligentsia (Russian)
sauna (Finnish)
taboo (Tongan)
thug (Hindi)
tycoon (Japanese)

English has also borrowed words from closer to home, for example, from Scottish Gaelic, including:

English	Gaelic	Meaning
bard	*bard*	poet
bog	*bog*	soft, wet
brogue	*bròg*	shoe
caber	*cabar*	pole
claymore	*claidheamh mòr*	big sword
dune	*dùn*	heap
galore	*gu leòr*	plenty

British English is still borrowing from other languages. In the global village, new words rush into English within a matter of weeks, especially whenever there's some upheaval in a foreign land. Most recently, a number of Arabic or Islamic terms – such as **fatwa**, **intifada** and **jihad** – have been adopted and adapted for domestic consumption.

CLASS OF '66

After the Norman conquest of England, a strict hierarchy developed. At the top was the monarch, below that the nobles (barons, bishops, dukes and earls), then knights and lords, and at the bottom were peasants or **serfs**, effectively indentured labourers. This hierarchy, known as the **feudal system**, was the basis of the class system which still exists in Britain today.

You say toe-may-toe, I say tow-mah-tow

Alongside the constant shifts in vocabulary, the English accent keeps on developing too. The clipped vowels and consonants of 1930s newsreels are a thing of the past, but even the voices on TV and radio 20 years ago sound dated today.

A notable development in the 1960s was the rise of **Estuary English**, a hybrid dialect between the original **cockney** of London and standard English. It's called 'Estuary' because it developed with the new towns along the banks of the Thames Estuary to the east of London. Today, Estuary English is very widely spoken across much of south and southeast England, and has given English such phrases as **Wasssamatter wiv yer?** (What's wrong with you?) and **ain't never dun nuffing** (I haven't done anything).

> "WASSSAMATTER WIV YER?
> – WHAT'S WRONG WITH YOU?"

An even more recent trend of spoken British English is the tendency to end statements with an upward inflection, making them sound like questions. This rising intonation is thought to have been introduced from Australian and New Zealand English, where it's common, via popular Australian soap operas such as *Neighbours* and *Home and Away*.

What's in a word?

The key features of the English language include words lifted from elsewhere, multiple alternative words with the same meaning, flexibility and simplification. This section looks at some of these aspects in more detail, as they help explain many of the modern developments in British English.

STATION TO STATION

The word **Charing** in the name of London's Charing Cross train station derives from a borrowed French term, *Chère Reine*, meaning 'dear queen'. When King Edward I's wife Eleanor died in 1290, the grief-stricken monarch ordered memorial crosses to be placed everywhere her funeral procession rested on its way from Nottinghamshire to London. One of these points was Charing Cross – a reproduction cross stands in the courtyard of the station today.

Language on loan

Borrowing (a polite way of saying pilfering) words is a major feature of the English language - in fact, it is generally believed that English contains more loanwords than any other language. It tends to occur when existing words are inadequate or too restricting. For example, English is happy with Anglo-Saxon terms for the basics of building (**brick**, **door**, **roof**, **wall**, **window**), but for the finer points of architecture it has turned to Italian - **capital**, **corridor**, **cupola**, **dome**, **mezzanine**, **portico**.

Once foreign words are imported, English takes what seems to be a random approach to their pronunciation.

Many foreign words keep their original pronunciation, or something like it. For example, British English speakers follow the French pronunciation for **parquet** and **rendezvous** (pronounced 'parkay' and 'rondayvoo'). But for the word **repartee** the Brits ignore the French and pronounce it as 'repartee', not 'repartay'. (Confusingly, in American English it's pronounced 'repartay')

Similarly, British English has borrowed the word **marijuana** from Spanish without altering the spelling or pronunciation very much, but the word **guerrilla** is nearly always pronounced

'gerila' (not 'gereelya' as in Spanish) – which doesn't help distinguish freedom fighters from large primates. Other Spanish words have been totally anglicised – *cucaracha* and *cocodrilo*, for example, have become **cockroach** and **crocodile**. Sometimes the Brits can't even decide which pronunciation to favour. For example, the first letter of the word **junta** can be pronounced both *j* (as in 'junk') and *h* (as in 'hunt' – from the Spanish pronunciation).

A wealth of words

The English language is in love with words and there's often a choice between a simple native English word and another one of foreign origin which expresses a different nuance of meaning. For example, you can choose to **make** something (from Old English), or there's always the option of using **manufacture** (Latin via Italian) or **synthesise** (Greek) instead. You can **speak** or **say** something (Old English) or, if you want to be taken more seriously, you can **communicate** or **converse** (Latin). Latin and Greek were the languages of education for centuries and they still have erudite overtones. There are many instances where an English noun has a Latin adjective – as in **earth** and **terrestrial**, **horse** and **equestrian**.

FEELING SHEEPISH

One of the few relics of the Old English system of inflection (see p21) is plurals such as **children**, **men**, **women** and **feet**. And then there are the odd ones – **deer**, **fish**, **sheep** – that don't have a separate plural form at all, and seem to be there for no other reason than to make foreigners look stupid when they say 'sheeps'.

A play on words

The flexibility and sheer size of the English lexicon, with numerous words for the same thing and numerous words sounding the same, means wordplay has been a major feature of the language for centuries.

Fourteenth-century writer Chaucer certainly took advantage, as did Shakespeare who alone is credited with creating hundreds of idioms (such as **cold comfort**, **cruel to be kind**, **foul play**, **mind's eye**, **one fell swoop**, **poisoned chalice**) which have remained in everyday use for 400 years.

DO YOU GET IT?

One of the greatest achievements of the simplification of the English language was the invention of the phrasal verb – the combination of a verb and a preposition or adverb to achieve a new meaning.

The word **get** is the best example. It's an Old English survivor with a basic meaning of 'obtain', but this is only its part-time job. It spends the rest of its life joined to other words creating phrasal verbs and a host of new meanings.

You **get up** and **get out of** bed, and remember you **got out of** your head last night again – which is **getting to be** a drag because it makes it so hard **to get started** in the mornings.

Phrasal verbs today form the basis of everyday speech and are the key to the structural simplicity of the language. They're also the bane of foreign students learning English, firstly because there are so many of them and secondly because they have to be learned by heart. There's no way you could deduce that you **get on** and **get off** a train, boat or plane, but **get in** and **get out of** a car.

> “COLD COMFORT, FOUL PLAY, MIND'S EYE
> – PHRASES COINED BY SHAKESPEARE”

Many other expressions entered the language from the Authorised or King James Version of the Bible, translated in the 17th century, and are still with us today, including **salt of the earth**, **skin of your teeth**, **sour grapes** and **suffer fools gladly**.

As well as wordplay and idioms, English can produce new terms simply by combining old ones or placing them side by side. For example, tabloid newspapers are responsible for an entire shorthand vocabulary such as **drug fiend**, **gymslip mum**, **love rat**, **porn king**, **sex romp** or **tug-of-love child**.

Keeping it simple

While English has ceaselessly expanded its vocabulary, it has also simplified its grammar, stripping down the engine of language to basic components wherever possible.

Old English was an 'inflected' language, with words changing form depending on the tense, their function and the relationship between the person speaking and the person addressed. Like modern German, Old English had three genders. Nouns had numerous 'cases' (different forms depending on their function in a sentence), and there were as many as 11 forms of adjectives. By the end of the 14th century, however, English had simply dumped most of the complex inflections, cases and genders.

Instead of having the word-ending change to clarify how a word related to others in a sentence, English now employs a range of simple prepositions – **at**, **from**, **in**, **to**, **with**.

Gender was simply dropped. Does it add anything to a language to give a crankshaft or an omelette a gender? Not really. So English uses just 'a' and 'the', not pairs like *un* and *une*

and *le* and *la* as in French, and most nouns (apart from things like bulls and cows) are refreshingly neutral.

In the same way, English has sometimes dispensed with words that make no useful distinction. For example, French feels it necessary to distinguish between 'to know' in the sense of acquaintance (*connaître*) – 'I know Charlie very well' – and 'to know' in the sense of knowledge (*savoir*) – 'I know how to play the piano'. English is content with the one verb.

In French you say 'I am (*être*) a woman' but 'I have (*avoir*) hunger', but English considers such distinctions unnecessary and assumes that people saying 'I'm thirsty' will not be misunderstood as meaning they will always be thirsty. However, just to keep everyone on their toes, English *does* feel a need to distinguish between other things, like **hearing** and **listening**, or **looking** and **seeing**.

Another clever trick is to employ an army of simple prefixes and suffixes (for example **dis-**, **pre-**, **re-**, **-y**) to alter the sense of a word. Negation can be expressed through the application of **a-**, **anti-**, **il-**, **in-**, **ir-**, **non-**, **un**. Adjectives can be converted to nouns using **-ness**, nouns into adjectives using **-ible**, and adverbs created using **-ably**.

Standard English has also done away with informal and formal forms of address. In German, there are seven forms of the word 'you'. In English, you don't have to worry about where you stand in relation to someone else or what degree of respect they should be shown – everyone is simply **you**. English is very economical in its use of definite or indefinite articles, too: you can say 'I'm going to bed' or 'I don't want lunch' or 'It's Derby day', where other languages would require articles (*the* bed, *the* lunch, *the* day of the Derby).

All change

Another aspect of English is its tendency to let the same word do service as a noun or a verb (eg **drink**, **love**, **push**, **smoke**). Its versatility also allows English to make one word from two

METAPHORICALLY SPEAKING

The English language has a special love affair with metaphor. Every industry, every sport, every form of endeavour generates its own vocabulary, and as soon as this happens it's mined for metaphors.

Take, for example, the military and naval spheres. Before you even start to **drum up** support for your **campaign**, you must **nail your colours to the mast**. Then you need to **set your sights** on a **united front**, **steering clear** of **loose cannons** or **camp followers** and anyone likely to **break ranks** under their **baptism of fire**.

And that's only a start. Even if you've never been involved in the sports of boxing or wrestling, you may still have **stepped into the ring** or found yourself **on the ropes**, **talking a good fight** but unable to **box clever** and forced to **slug it out** with some **heavyweight** who doesn't **pull their punches**.

In the same way, hunting has given us **cut to the chase**, **open season**, **sitting duck** and **stalking horse**. From the animal kingdom comes **a game of cat and mouse**, **penguin suit**, **snake in the grass**, **stubborn as a mule** and **mad as a box of frogs**. Even plant-life has supplied **lily-livered**, **pansy**, **shrinking violet** and **wallflower**.

(**coathanger**, **doorknob**, **handbook**) – although only to form simple compounds. Long or unwieldy compounds such as those favoured by German (like *Gewerkschaftsbewegung*, meaning 'trade union movement') generally don't appear.

WHEN MORE IS MORE

To the question, 'How many words do you need?', English replies, 'How many have you got?' It never seems to have enough. Calculations vary according to how 'an English word' is defined, but range from about 100,000 to over a million. The *Oxford English Dictionary* contains around 600,000 words.

Around 1950, linguists produced Basic English, a stripped-down version of the language with a vocabulary of just 850 words. There's nothing you can't say in Basic English, but that hasn't stopped anyone using the other 599,150.

One problem with versatility, however, is inconsistency. Take the adjectival form of nouns. Here's what looks like a nice simple pattern:

clamour clamorous
glamour glamorous
humour humorous

But look what happens elsewhere:

colour colourful
favour favourite
savour savoury
splendour splendid

Despite wonderful simplifications in some areas, English sometimes seems to play about with words for no particular reason.

SPEAKING BRITISH ENGLISH

Raining cats & dogs

Look out for these...

CLASSIC PHRASE:

RAINING CATS AND DOGS

A popular way of saying it's pouring with rain – and thus commonly heard

TRY THIS ONE:

CHATTERING ON THE BLOWER

The blower is an antiquated name for a phone, hence talking on the phone

USE WITH CAUTION:

'YOU LOOKING FOR TROUBLE OR CHEWING GRAVEL?'

Meaning 'you might meet the end of this encounter with a punch in the mouth'

MISUNDERSTANDINGS:

'WITH ALL DUE RESPECT'

Actually means 'I have no respect for your view'

SPEAKING BRITISH ENGLISH

This chapter will guide you through some of the quirks of British English grammar and pronunciation, then delve deeper into the peculiarities of etiquette, body language and conversations about that most British of topics – the weather.

Minding your p's & q's

As seen in the Short History chapter, a major feature of the English language is its propensity to borrow words from other languages around the world. The English language has also travelled abroad over the centuries – to Australasia, the Americas, India, parts of Africa, the Caribbean and many more places – and developed separately in each area.

The result: the same words are often pronounced differently in Britain and in other English-speaking countries. The difference may lie in which syllable of a word is emphasised, how a vowel is pronounced, or even which consonant is used.

The selection of everyday English words given below have the same spelling and the same meaning in Britain, Australia, America and other English-speaking countries, but are pronounced differently.

"WATCHA

– HELLO"

borough	the British English pronunciation is 'burah', not 'buroh'
clerk	pronounced 'clark'
decade	*de*cade (not 'de*cade*')
era	'eera', the first syllable rhymes with 'ear' (it is not pronounced 'airah', as in the US)
fillet	'fillet' (the *t* is pronounced)
glacial	'glayshul' – the first *a* is pronounced to rhyme with 'hay'
glacier	'glasier' – the *a* pronounced as in 'crass'
herb	the *h* is pronounced in British English
hostel	'*ho*stul' – the second syllable is not the same as in 'hotel'
hostile	'hostyle' – the second syllable rhymes with 'style' (also in **sterile** and **fertile**)
medicine	often 'medsin' – notice, only two syllables
nauseous	'nawseus' – three syllables, not two as in American English
pasta	'pasta' – the first syllable rhymes with 'mass'
penchant	pronounced like the French, 'ponshon'
privacy	'privasee' – the *i* pronounced as in 'bit'
schedule	'shedyual' – not 'skedyual' as in American English
sexual	'seksyual' or 'sekshual'
urinal	'yurainal' – the *i* pronounced as in 'wine'
vaginal	'vajainal' – the *i* as in 'wine'
vitamin	'vitamin' – *i* pronounced as in 'fit'

ROUTE OR ROUT?

The word **route**, as in 'the route from London to Brighton', is pronounced 'root' in British English. In American English, it's spelt 'route' but usually pronounced to rhyme with 'pout' (although in some parts of New England the British pronunciation is still favoured). The word **rout** – ie, a crushing defeat – is pronounced to rhyme with 'pout' in both British and American English. To add to the confusion, the first syllable of **router**, a woodworking implement, also rhymes with 'pout' in both British and American English. Then there's the **router**, a computer peripheral. Some British techies pronounce it 'rooter', to distinguish it from the carpenter's tool, while others favour the rhyme-with-'pout' option, influenced perhaps by American colleagues.

yoghurt	'yoghurt' – *o* pronounced as in 'hot'
z	the letter *z* is pronounced 'zed', not 'zee' as in the US
zebra	'zebra' to rhyme with 'Debra'

Speaking proper-like

The grammar of standard British English doesn't differ much from the grammar of other varieties of the English language, such as US English and Australian English, and there's very little that's likely to cause misunderstandings. Dialects of British English that do use different grammar rules are discussed in the Regional Variations chapter.

Spellbound

One of the most noticeable differences between the varieties of English is the divide between British English spelling and American English spelling. For example, in Britain, the preferred spelling is **-tre** (not **-ter**):

centre

litre

metre

theatre

Likewise, many words end in **-our**, not **-or**, in British:

colour

endeavour

honour

labour

neighbour

savour

And words which end in **-ize** in the US are generally spelt **-ise** in British English; for example:

aggrandise

finalise

pluralise

terrorise

Other words in British English which are spelt differently in other versions of English (especially in American English) include:

aluminium the US version is spelt 'aluminum', with four syllables and the stress on the second ('a*loo*minum'). The British use five syllables ('aloo*min*eeum') or four ('aloom-*in*yum') with the stress on the third.

SORTED FOR E'S

In English, not only are the same letters often pronounced differently, but the same sounds can be written several different ways. There are at least 11 different ways of writing the sound 'ee' in English, including:

donkey	Leigh	mummy	paediatrician
peep	people	piece	read
receive	reiterate	speciality	

Part of the problem is that English has a habit of borrowing words from other languages and retaining their spelling, but attempts to rationalise English spelling have been passionately resisted. People in Britain still get hot and bothered about the American practice of dropping the *u* from words such as 'colour' and 'glamour'. Indeed, there's nothing like an innocent Americanism to make most Brits turn purple.

defence spelt 'defense' in the US (although **defensive** has an 's' in British English)

draught this word is pronounced 'draft' and relates to the verb 'to draw' meaning 'to pull' – as in a **draught horse** (a horse that pulls things) and **draught beer** (pulled from the barrel by a pump). It can also mean **draught** as in a light air current in a room ('It's draughty in here'). The British use the spelling **draft** to mean: 'to conscript' (**to draft someone into the army**); a document used to withdraw money at a bank; and a version of an essay or report (eg a **first draft**).

furore this is the British equivalent of the American word 'furor'. It's pronounced 'fyuroree' in three syllables.

gaol meaning 'jail' and pronounced that way

kerb British English spelling for 'curb' when it relates to a raised edge on a road. **Curb** means 'cut back' in British English.

WHAT'S THAT?

Many British people, especially in northern England, use **that** where other English speakers would use 'so' (eg 'The show was that boring, half the audience went to sleep').

programme pronounced the same as 'program' is in America

speciality notice the extra *i* making it five syllables – 'spe-shee-a-li-ty'

tonne a metric tonne – 1000kg. The imperial ton (2240lb or 1016kg) is also used in Britain – and not everyone knows the difference. (Both **ton** and **tonne** are pronounced 'tun' in British English.) Neither should be confused with the US 'short ton' (2000lb).

A turn of phrase

British English has some differences in phrasing compared to other English-speaking countries, where one word – usually a preposition – is different. Below are a few examples.

about some British English speakers may say 'I looked about me' as an alternative to 'I looked around me'

after in British English, to **ask after someone** is to ask about someone ('I met Jill today, she asked after you')

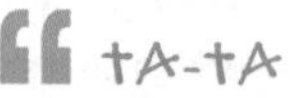

“TA-TA

— GOODBYE”

down to this means 'the responsibility of' (eg 'It's a good plan, but it's down to the teachers to make it work'). It's not the same as **up to you** – see below.

on heat of an animal, to be in season or in heat ('The cat's on heat')

up to a phrase that implies a choice ('Stay there, or come with us, it's up to you')

Body language

The main feature of British body language is its restraint! When speaking, most Brits are not very effusive or flamboyant, and they generally don't touch the people they're speaking to in the way some other cultures might find usual. (A hand on the arm to emphasise a point, for example, or continued gripping of hands after a handshake to emphasise friendship.) Exceptions of course include late nights in the pub when deep embraces and declarations along the lines of 'You're my besht mate, you are' seem perfectly normal.

Not only is touching and gesticulating generally avoided, but compared to many other cultures the Brits prefer to have a bit of space around them during a conversation. Standing too close can be misinterpreted as odd or simply forward. And

PREPOSITIONAL ANGST

'I will write you' makes British people wince. Brits prefer 'I will write to you', even though they're perfectly happy with 'I will phone you'. Americans say 'he took it in stride' rather than 'he took it in his stride', and 'she won't commit' as an alternative to 'she won't commit herself'. Cue more purple rage on the east side of the Atlantic.

anyone who looks you in the eye too much during a casual chat is definitely **suspect** (ie suspicious).

Handshaking is also restricted in Britain compared to many other cultures. It's usual when two people are being introduced to each other by a third person in a business situation, but is unusual among friends in everyday situations. Also, compared to their continental neighbours, it is extremely rare for British people to kiss strangers or casual acquaintances. However, among friends kissing on the cheek and **air kissing** – where the lips don't actually touch the skin – have become a lot more common and have led to the phrase **mwah, mwah** (duplicating the sound of the air kiss).

> "MWAH MWAH
> – AIR KISSING, BELOVED BY FASHIONABLE FOLKS"

Finally, there's the topic of volume. Brits generally speak more quietly in public than folks from many other cultures. On the London Underground it's not unusual for complete strangers to raise eyebrows in mutual amusement when booming American can be heard from the other end of the carriage. The exception is, of course, when Brits are on their mobile phones – then they're as loud as everyone else.

Watcha, me old mucker!

You'll hear numerous colloquial variations on the popular 'hi' around Britain, depending on where you are and who's talking to you.

For instance, in London and the south you'll often hear **Watcha**, while in some northern areas of England you might hear people say **Ay up** as a casual greeting (often pronounced 'ayoop') and **Ta-ra** for 'goodbye' (pronounced 'tarah').

Elsewhere in England you might hear **Ow do?**, an abbreviation of 'How do you do?', or simply **How?** or **Now then**. The 'goodbye' phrase may be something like **Ta-ta** or **Ta-da**. **Cheers** is also widely used to mean 'goodbye'.

In many areas, including the Midlands, northern England and the southwest, people passing each other on the street say **Are you all right?**, often reduced to **All right?** (this is pronounced differently in different regions: 'all roit' in the southwest; 'oroit' in the Midlands; 'aal reet' further north). The reply to this question is also **All right**, either as a statement (meaning 'Yes, I'm well thank you') or **All right?** as a question (ie 'I'm well thanks, and how are you?').

If you're greeted with a regional expression you're unfamiliar with in Britain, it's usually best to just say 'hello' or 'hi' in return. If you feel obliged to answer the apparent question, just say 'Fine, thanks' (in the same way as you always reply in the affirmative when people say 'How are you?', even if you've got a broken leg). Attempts to use the local vernacular may be interpreted as mockery, and in extreme cases you might end up **chewing gravel** (meaning 'reach the end of the encounter with a punch in the mouth' - from the witty challenge **You looking for trouble or chewing gravel? Either way you'll lose your teeth**).

> "CHEWING GRAVEL
> — BEING PUNCHED IN THE MOUTH"

Etiquette

Proper little madams

When speaking to strangers, or in formal situations, the most common terms of address are **Mr** and **Mrs**. The term **Miss** originally meant an unmarried woman, but is now used for young women. The neutral term **Ms**, although used by professional women in large cities, is less common in the wider population.

The British have a reputation for being reserved, and the use of Mr or Mrs is common with strangers or on first meeting. This is not to say first names are never used, but it's a good rule not to use a person's first name unless you've been invited to or that's the way they've been introduced. Even when you're a patron or customer, formal address is more common.

> "ME OLD LOVER
> — REFERS TO A FRIEND, NOT A FORMER ROMANTIC RELATIONSHIP"

Here are some other terms of address used around Britain:

chuck mainly used in Liverpool, Manchester and mid-Yorkshire, chuck is interchangeable with love (see below)

guv(ner) from 'governor', an informal yet respectful term of address for an owner or boss. It can also be used with irony.

love/luvvie a term of casual or friendly address. Although this is still common when speaking to members of the opposite sex, or between women, it can be construed as sexist and should never be used in a formal or professional setting. In Bristol and the southwest, the term **lover** or **old lover** is sometimes used, as in 'How are you, me old lover?'

This is not flirtatious, nor a reference to a former romantic relationship.

madam/sir both are still used by staff when serving customers

mate/matey used in casual address, as in 'Hey, mate, can you move your van?' The term is not restricted to men.

Titles for titles

Just in case you're ever invited to tea with the Queen, or find yourself **hob-nobbing** with high-borns, here are the correct terms of address to use:

Your Majesty	the king or queen. On presentation to the Queen, the correct formal address is 'Your Majesty' and subsequently 'Ma'am' (pronounced to rhyme with 'ham').
Your Royal Highness	the monarch's spouse, children, sisters and brothers
Your Highness	the monarch's nephews, nieces and cousins
Your Grace	a duke or duchess (also an Anglican archbishop)
Lord/Lady	those below the rank of duke/duchess (ie marquis/marchioness, earl/countess, viscount/viscountess, baron/baroness)

> "HOB-NOBBING – FRATERNISING WITH THE ELITE"

Please & thank you

Compared to English-speakers from other countries, the British can appear somewhat overzealous in the use of **please**. Elsewhere, a sign in a shop would read 'Pay Here' – in Britain, it's 'Please Pay Here'. Cashiers, after ringing up your items, will always state the amount you owe followed by the word please, as in 'Two pounds, please', even if you already know how much you owe and are extending it to them in your hand. They aren't being rude or unobservant, just stating the amount, and the please automatically comes with it.

It's the same with **thank you**. It would appear that many Brits simply can't say it too often. In less formal situations you'll hear **ta** (pronounced 'tar' or 'tah') or **cheers** instead of thank you.

Sorry?

As well as being used in apologies, the word **sorry** is used to mean 'What did you say?' – in the same way as you might say 'Pardon?' or 'Excuse me?' You'll also normally hear sorry in

READING BETWEEN THE LINES

In British English, as in some other languages, opening phrases are not always as they appear. Below are some common phrases, and their more honest translations.

Far be it from me to say, but...
I'm determined you'll hear my opinion

With all due respect...
I have no respect for your view

No offence intended...
This may offend you, but I don't care

ON THE BLOWER

A slang term for the phone is the **blower**, which harks back to the days when telephone mouthpieces were shaped like a horn. In London and the South, you might **get on the dog** to make a call. It's short for **dog and bone** – cockney rhyming slang for 'phone' (see p152 for more).

Britain instead of 'Pardon me' or 'Excuse me' when someone needs to get past you (in the street or a cinema, for example).

Telephone

In England a mobile phone is called simply that, a mobile (what Americans refer to as 'cell' phones). So you'll often hear 'Call me on my mobile'. Here are some translated British English telephone terms to help you avoid possible confusion:

directory enquiries telephone information service

engaged this means the line is occupied, or 'busy'. People don't use the term 'busy signal'; they simply say 'I can't get through, the line's engaged'.

ex-directory unlisted number

ring the British ring (or **ring up**) people, rather than 'call' them (eg 'I'll ring you tonight')

Who is that? the equivalent of 'Who's there?' or 'Who's calling?' (note, not 'Who's this?' as in American and Australian English)

The weather forecast

As a nation the Brits are obsessed with the weather, which is mainly because the weather is notoriously changeable. It can be warm and sunny in the morning, then snowing by lunchtime. In towns and cities, in the rare cases that Brits speak to strangers, chances are it'll be about the weather.

THEY'RE NOT QUESTIONS, INNIT?

The quintessentially British expressions **isn't it?** and **didn't it?** (or **didn't she?**, **isn't he?**, **didn't they?** and so on) are tacked on to the end of a surprisingly large number of statements – turning them unexpectedly into questions. It can be confusing for foreigners. The commonly heard **innit** originally derived from 'isn't it?'. However, it has now become a catchall tag you will hear at the end of any sentence, in a similar way people used to say 'you know': 'I'm going down the pub, innit' or 'I met her at school, innit.'

It can seem as though the British speaker is seeking corroboration on things you couldn't possibly know: 'I had a date with Steve last night, and I spilled a drink all over him, didn't I?' The custom reaches new heights when used as a snappish retort. Friends might say: 'John, we've been waiting for an hour.' John's annoyed reply: 'I was stuck in traffic, wasn't I?'

These aren't real questions. The trick when replying to one is to focus on the main statement, and reply as usual – 'Oh, really' or 'Oh no, what a shame', as appropriate. If in doubt, remember the golden rule: it's not really a question, is it?

“What a scorcher! – an extremely hot day”

In the countryside a casual nod or quick hello in passing is not unusual even between strangers, but once again any other conversation is likely to be about the weather and the Brits never seem to be happier than when complaining about it. If it's not too wet, it's too dry, and if it's not too hot, it's too cold.

Some other weather-related terms:

cutting	very cold ('That wind is cutting' – used in eastern England)
drizzle	light rain
fret	sea mist (in northeast England)
lashing	raining heavily ('It's lashing down')
mizzle	a mix of light rain and mist
muggy	humid
perishing	freezing
raining cats and dogs	raining hard
scorcher	extremely hot day

LIVING LIFE – THE BRITISH WAY

Zebra crossing

CLASSIC PHRASE:

WHAT A WEE BONNIE BAIRN

In Scotland, the way to compliment a parent on having a very attractive little baby

TRY THIS ONE:

IT'S ALL GONE PEAR-SHAPED

The thing to say when things go horribly wrong

USE WITH CAUTION:

'STEVE'S HAVING A WHIZZ IN THE CRAPPER'

A rather indelicate way of saying 'Steve is having a pee in the toilet'

MISUNDERSTANDINGS:

CABINET

Not a cupboard, but the key decision-making body of the British Government

LIVING LIFE – THE BRITISH WAY

At home, at work or at school, or while travelling in the town or in the country, there are a host of British English words and phrases that might not be understood by English speakers from abroad.

Flats, bedsits & semis

Types of dwelling

It's not a big place, so Britain can seem crowded at times, with the inhabitants living **cheek by jowl** (close to one another) in **flats**, **bedsits** or **semis**.

If those words don't confuse you, there are many others which might! Below is a selection of terms to describe homes and houses, and the rooms within them.

bedsit short for **bedsitting room**, literally a single room for living and sleeping, usually in a large house converted into several bedsits. As housing stock is replaced, bedsits, like **tenements**, are becoming rarer as they get knocked down.

bungalow any single-storey house

council house house built by a town or city council, often with subsidised rent

detached house a free-standing house (not joined to any other). The word is generally used in an urban environment. A lonely cottage in the country would not usually be referred to as a detached house.

digs colloquial term for lodgings or a place to stay (usually short term)

estate a large area of land held by one person or family. See also **housing estate**.

flat dwelling in part of a larger building, usually – but not always – on one level. Called an 'apartment' in the US. The larger building usually contains many other flats. A very large building containing many flats is called a **block of flats** (same as an 'apartment block' in the US).

housing estate group of houses, from a few to several hundred, planned and built by a town council or private developer. On some housing estates, new schools, shops and community facilities are also built.

maisonette when a large house is divided into two (or more) separate dwellings, one on each floor, the term maisonette is sometimes used instead of **flat**

semi-detached house two houses joined by a common wall, but otherwise standing alone (often shortened to semi)

studio flat slightly more up-market and larger than a bedsit, but again, a single room for living and sleeping

tenement especially in Scotland, this is a term for a rundown block of flats in a poor area of town

terraced houses row of houses, usually all built to the same plan and attached to one another

Around the house

Visitors from overseas may find familiar objects with very unfamiliar names inside the typical British house. (For terms used in specific regions, see the Regional Variations chapter.)

> “CRAPPER, BOG, LAV
>
> – TOILET”

" WHIZZ, PISS, SLASH
– URINATE "

bath what Americans call 'the bathtub'. Where the British might say 'He's in the bath', Americans would say 'He's in the tub'.

bin where the household **rubbish** ('trash' to Americans) goes, usually indoors (eg 'Put it in the bin under the sink'). Bin is often used as a verb: 'Bin it' means 'Throw it away'.

cling film transparent food wrap; called 'Saran Wrap' or 'cellophane' in US English and 'Glad Wrap' or 'cling wrap' in Australian English

cutlery eating utensils such as knives and forks; 'silverware' in the US

dishcloth in British English, this is the small cloth used for doing the **washing up**; it's called a 'dishrag' in US English. The larger cloth used for drying clean dishes is called a **tea towel** in British English (and a 'dishcloth' in US English).

dustbin large receptacle for rubbish, usually kept outside; called a 'garbage bin' or 'trash can' in the US

duvet (pronounced 'doovay') a warm quilt covering a bed, with a removable (washable) cover, meaning no top sheets or blankets are required. Called a 'doona' in Australian English, and sometimes called a 'comforter' in US English. If it lies on top of sheets and blankets and doesn't have a removable cover then it's called a **quilt** or **eiderdown** in British English.

grill **to grill** means to cook under electric coils or a gas flame. **The grill** is usually in or above the oven; it's called a 'broiler' in US English. What Americans call 'the grill' (the cooker in the back yard) is called a **barbecue** in British English.

jug receptacle for carrying or pouring liquids; 'pitcher' in the US. (**Jugs** is also vulgar slang for breasts.)

kettle receptacle used for boiling water to make tea or coffee. Occasionally called a **tea kettle**.

lodger a person who rents one room in a house that's otherwise owned and occupied by someone else

lounge living room; sitting room

skip large metal receptacle for carrying away rubbish (after building work, for example); sometimes called a 'dumpster' in US English

tap device for turning water on and off; called a 'faucet' or 'spigot' in the US

tenant a person who rents a house or apartment (when the house owner usually lives elsewhere)

wardrobe what Americans call a 'clothes closet'. This can be a moveable piece of furniture or 'built-in'.

wheelie bin outdoor rubbish bin on wheels

Kith & kin

Parents in Britain are usually known as **mum** and **dad** (or **mummy** and **daddy** by young children, and by daughters of any age in well-to-do families). Note the spelling: it's not 'mom' and 'mommy' as in the US.

Grandparents are usually called **grandad** or **grandpa** and **grandma** or **granny** (or simply **gran**). Another common term for grandmother is **nan** or **nana** – the latter favoured by young children.

Auntie is the diminutive of **aunt** used by young children. **Uncle** remains **uncle**. Both terms are sometimes given by children to adult friends of their parent/s, even if there's no blood relationship.

TOILET TROUBLE

The **toilet** in British English is also called the **lavatory** or **WC** – although both those terms are pretty dated. It's perfectly acceptable (even preferable in some circles) to call it the **loo**. Toilet means both the actual object (so a plumber might 'fit a new toilet') and the room (so you might 'leave the table to visit the toilet'). In Britain, people don't use the euphemism 'bathroom'. These days advertisers come right out and sell you **toilet paper**, not 'bathroom tissue', too.

In pubs and restaurants you'll see signs for **Ladies** and **Gents**. The many less charming British slang terms for the toilet include the **crapper**, **bog** and **lavvy**. The equivalent of the Aussie 'dunny' (ie a toilet in a separate building in the garden rather than in the house) is **privy**. US terms such as 'john' or the 'can' are rarely used.

As to the action, while Americans speak of having to 'pee', the British are more likely to **wee**. Other slang terms include **whizz**, **piss** and **having a slash**.

Some other family-related words are:

bairn baby (in northern England and Scotland). Other terms for young children include **ankle-biter** and **tot**.

child-minder someone who looks after children during the day, usually on a regular (paid) basis at their own home or the home of the children (while the parent/s are at work). This term is generally not applied to employees at a **crèche** or **nursery**, both of which are places that look after babies and pre-school children.

cot small bed specifically for a baby or young child; called a 'crib' in US English

nappy absorbent underwear worn by children that haven't been toilet trained; called a 'diaper' in the US

pram effectively a small bed on wheels for babies that cannot yet sit up on their own in a **pushchair** (a small chair on wheels). The word is a shortened form of **perambulator**, meaning 'something you can walk with'.

> "BAIRN, TOT, ANKLE-BITER
> – CHILD"

Holidaying

A **holiday** means time off work or school – a 'vacation' in US English. People may say, for example, 'I'm taking a holiday in Spain this year' or 'I won't be at work next week – I'll be on holiday'. Places to stay or visit on holiday include:

bed and breakfast often shortened to **B&B**, this is essentially accommodation in a room (or rooms) in someone's house, and a truly great British institution

camp site an area where tents can be pitched and caravans parked. Called a 'campground' or 'camping site' in some other English-speaking countries.

inn technically, a **pub** with accommodation. It's a legal requirement in Britain for a place calling itself an inn to offer accommodation. That's why many pubs once called 'The Crown Inn' or 'The Oak Inn' are now called simply 'The Crown' or 'The Oak'.

seaside an area, usually a resort, beside the sea. When Brits plan a holiday, they say they're going to the seaside rather than to 'the ocean', or simply 'the sea'. Even if the resort is on the Atlantic Ocean, it's still called the seaside.

BRAND NAMES

In Britain, these brand names have become either totally or partly synonymous with the generic product:

Domestos	liquid bleach
Durex	condom
Hoover	vacuum cleaner
Land Rover	all-terrain vehicle
Nescafé	instant coffee
Savlon	antiseptic ointment
Sellotape	transparent adhesive tape
TCP	antiseptic liquid
Tipp-ex	correction fluid
WD-40	fine lubricant in a spray can
Zimmer frame	walking aid, usually for old people

staycation a holiday spent at home

theme park a funfair with roller coasters and other attractions. What Americans would call an 'amusement park'.

School days

There are regional variations but British education falls into three major stages:

primary school	for children aged around 5 to 11
secondary education	from around 11 years onward
tertiary education	university or college

This section covers some main components of the education system in Britain – although in some cases they apply to England only. The system in Wales is similar to England's, while Scotland has its own education system which differs in some areas.

There are many British English words and phrases to do with education which people from other English-speaking countries might not understand, so **sit up straight** and listen at the back, here are some guidelines:

A-levels short for 'Advanced levels' – examinations which students aspiring to go to university take, usually at around age 18, as entrance qualifications

A-S-levels exams taken a year before A-levels

college a college may be part of a university (like one of the colleges of Oxford or Cambridge) or a stand-alone educational establishment, either for students 16 to 18 (also called **sixth form college**) or for those over 18 – for example a teacher-training college or a technical college

comprehensive school a type of secondary school that's publicly funded and requires no special qualifications to enter (unlike a grammar school)

Free School the first Free Schools opened in September 2011. These schools are nonprofit-making, independent, state-funded schools, set up by a wide range of proposers – including charities, universities, businesses, educational groups, teachers or parents.

grammar school in the late Victorian era grammar schools were organised to provide academically-orientated secondary education throughout England and Wales. Today, 'grammar school' commonly refers to one of the few remaining fully selective state-funded schools in England and Northern Ireland.

Oxbridge the word for Oxford and Cambridge when speaking of the two universities together. A student joining one of these august institutions is said to be **going up to** Oxford or Cambridge.

public school a secondary school that (despite the name) is neither publicly funded nor open to the general public. A public school is a private or independent school, usually several centuries old, of high educational standard and costly to attend. Eton, Rugby, Harrow and Winchester are famous examples of public schools.

revise to study or prepare for an exam. Thus, when British students talk about **revising** they don't mean rewriting a paper, they mean studying (as in 'I have to stay in tonight and revise for my biology exam'). Also known as **cramming** from the American.

swot a slang term meaning to study intensively for an examination ('I stayed up all night to swot for my exams'). In British English a pupil who studies regularly might be called **a swot** disapprovingly by classmates.

tuition this word has several meanings: teaching, tutoring and lessons (whether private or class). Hence, **tuition fees** – the money students pay for their tertiary education.

"to swot – to study intensively"

Nine to five

Some job titles in British English are not the same as in other parts of the English-speaking world.

barrister a lawyer who argues cases in court (a **solicitor**, by contrast, prepares the client's case out of court)

caretaker what Americans call a 'janitor'

charlady old-fashioned term for a female cleaner

dustman garbage collector

farrier blacksmith who shoes horses

gaffer slang term meaning boss or foreman (possibly derived from Arabic *gaffier*, meaning 'guardian')

GP General Practitioner – a family doctor as opposed to a specialist or hospital doctor

newsagent both a person who works in a small newspaper shop and the shop itself

lollipop lady/man a guard at road crossings near schools, to stop traffic when children cross. The name comes from the large sign they carry to warn vehicles.

postman a man who collects or delivers the post (ie the mail). Although many postal workers are female, the term 'postman' is proving hard to shake – perhaps thanks partly to children's cartoon character Postman Pat.

publican owner or manager of a pub. Also called a **landlord**, irrespective of their actual ownership position.

solicitor see **barrister** (note that the sign 'No Solicitors', which you might see on office doors in America, is not used in Britain. The British equivalent is **No Hawkers** or **No Visitors Without an Appointment**.)

turf accountant a term used to describe a person who works at a betting shop – where you go to stake money on a horse race. (It's also a name for the betting shop itself.) The term may have been coined originally as a euphemism, but it's now a formal term – although not used so commonly these days.

vicar clergyman in the Anglican Church (Church of England)

Has it got legs?

In Britain, as elsewhere, office workers – and especially managers – have developed their own terminology; many of the British words are derived from American corporate-speak:

big ask tough or demanding ('This job has to be finished next week. It's a big ask, but everyone will have to work over the weekend.')

ducks in a row organised ('We're falling behind and really need our ducks in a row on this job'). Not to be confused with **cocks on the block** – meaning it's a major risk and there'll be serious damage if it fails.

face time a meeting or discussion in person, as opposed to on the phone

> "IT'S GONE PEAR-SHAPED – A DISASTER"

going forward in the future – much loved in office-speak. Mangled variations include 'in terms of going forward' and even 'going forward-wise'.

legs feasibility ('The plans look good, but has this project got legs?'). Other variations are **Will it run?** and **Will it fly?** If a plan seems unfeasible a sceptic might say 'It'll never fly'.

park to set aside a topic to be discussed later, so that the meeting or discussion can focus on the main issue. Variations are 'put it in long-term parking' or 'park it nearby, and keep the engine on'.

to go pear-shaped to have problems; to fail ('Things were going well, then the finance collapsed and it all went pear-shaped'.)

Love & marriage

The term 'dating' is not commonly used in Britain. People might **go on a date**, but once it gets regular the term **seeing** or **going out with** is used instead. Sometimes the old-fashioned term **courting** is used ironically – when the courting (in the sense of trying to win affection) is over, and the relationship is happening. Here are some other British love and dating terms you may encounter:

bonk to have sex, as in 'I'd bonk him/her'. Very similar to **shag**. Originally, a bonk just meant to strike or thump.

chat up to attempt to endear oneself. The US equivalent is 'come on to' or 'hit on'. A **chat-up line** is a 'smooth' opening line, the classic being 'Haven't I seen you somewhere before?' In Britain, being **chatted up** is okay, if you like the person who's doing the chatting up. It's not used as a derogatory or scathing term, as it might be in some other forms of English – well, not always.

cop off to meet someone, usually at a party or similar, and end the evening with sexual activity

crumpet attractive woman (the term is generally used by men). Also used as a plural: 'The lads were on the town, looking to pull crumpet'.

have it off slightly vulgar and immature way of describing sex ('They'd only just been introduced, but two hours later they were having it off in the back of a car')

playing away having an extramarital affair

pull when used as a verb, pull has a similar meaning as **cop off**. It can also be used as a noun; someone might be described as **a great pull**. Another version is **on the pull**; ie looking for a romantic or sexual encounter.

quickie this originally meant anything done quickly or in a hurry; it now means quick sex

“BONK, SHAG, HAVE IT OFF – TO HAVE SEX WITH”

randy slang term for feeling libidinous or aroused (used where Americans would use horny)

shag vulgar slang for sex (as in 'I had a great shag last night') and certainly not the name for a dance as it is in America. It is also used to define a person's sexual prowess: 'I met this guy; he was a great shag'. Hence also **shagger** (someone who shags a lot, or aims to) and **shagging** (eg 'John and Jane were caught shagging in the bathroom'). **Shagged** is also slang for 'very tired'.

snog a long kiss, especially in a teenage context. For example: 'John and Jane started the night having a snog in the broom-cupboard'. Also used as a verb: 'I'd really like to snog you'. Hence also **snogging**.

Yes, Prime Minister

The British Parliament calls itself the **Mother of Parliaments**, being one of the oldest in the world, and having exported its concepts to many other countries. Thus, some British terms relating to politics and government are also used in, say, India, Australia or the US. However, many other terms have remained unique to Britain. Here are some official and jargon terms that could be confusing if you're not familiar with British politics:

bill a draft act of parliament, to be debated by **MPs** and members of the **House of Lords**. When a bill is **passed** it becomes an **act of Parliament**, and the basis for law.

cabinet not a cupboard but the key decision-making body of government. Consists of the **Prime Minister** and ministers.

Chancellor of the Exchequer cabinet minister in charge of the national treasury (often called the 'Minister of Finance' in other countries). Not to be confused with the **Lord Chancellor**.

Conservative Party right-of-centre political party, one of the two major parties in British politics. Also called the **Tory Party**.

dissemble an obscure term which entered political jargon when an **MP** found himself unable to say he'd previously lied to his colleagues; instead he said he'd **dissembled** the facts. MPs are not allowed to accuse one another of lying during debates in the **House of Commons**. (If they do, they're evicted by the **Speaker**.)

Downing Street Number 10 Downing Street in London is the official residence of the Prime Minister, and Number 11 is the official residence of the Chancellor of the Exchequer. Hence Downing Street and **Number 10** are terms often used synonymously with 'the Government'.

Eurosceptic a politician opposed to Britain's ties with the European Union

filibuster to speak for an unnecessarily long period, to deliberately waste time so that a parliamentary debate ends without conclusion: effectively a technique for preventing a **bill** becoming an **act**

House of Commons the lower house of Parliament, consisting of around 600 elected **Members of Parliament (MPs)**

House of Lords the upper house of Parliament; currently an unelected body composed of nobles, appointed peers and high-ranking clergy

Labour Party centre-left political party, one of the two major parties in British politics

Liberal Democrats centrist party, third-strongest in Britain; often shortened to Lib-Dems

Lord Chancellor more formally called the **Lord High Chancellor**, the head of the judiciary and senior figure in the **House of Lords**

MP abbreviation for **Member of Parliament** (ie a member of the **House of Commons**)

MSP a Member of the Scottish Parliament

the Opposition more formally called **Her/His Majesty's Loyal Opposition**, this refers to the principal party opposing the governing party in the British Parliament

Prime Minister the head of the government, usually the leader of the party holding the majority of seats in the **House of Commons**. (There are not separate elections for the Prime Minister in Britain, as there are for presidents and other heads of state in some other countries – the British head of state is the monarch.)

Speaker key figure in the **House of Commons**; the Speaker keeps order during debates, calls on **MPs** to make speeches and casts the deciding vote in the case of ties

spin a shorthand term for a message from the government where positives are emphasised or negatives hidden, and by extension for political manipulation of the media. Lazy journalists imply that spin is a modern phenomenon, but rulers and governments have engaged in spin since the days of Ancient Egypt – and possibly longer. The word has now entered mainstream vocabulary – a company director may be accused by shareholders of **spinning** a report on lacklustre financial results, for example.

Westminster the formal name for the Houses of Parliament in London is the **Palace of Westminster**, and so the term Westminster is also used to refer to Parliament. (The Palace of Westminster is in the City of Westminster, a separate city within London.)

Town & country

Britain is, as the brochures say, a land of contrasts. In between the towns and cities are large areas of open countryside. Well, they're large by British standards, although visitors used to the Australian Outback or Alaska may not agree...

Going down town

Most urban settlements in Britain are towns. In fact the name comes from **tun**, an Old English term meaning 'an enclosed or fortified village', remembered today by the numerous place names ending in **-ton** – Southampton, Workington, Weston and so on. Today in Britain a town can have anything from several hundred inhabitants to several thousand. Essentially, it's larger than a village and smaller than a city – although there are a few exceptions. This section covers some British phrases relating to towns and other urban areas.

borough an urban community (technically one that has been 'incorporated' by royal charter), either standing alone (many market towns across England are boroughs) or forming part of a city (London has 32 boroughs). The word is derived from the Old English word **burg** (meaning 'fortified town').

city a very large urban settlement, such as London, Manchester, Birmingham, Edinburgh, Glasgow or Cardiff. Generally, the British definition of a city differs from the American. British cities generally have several hundred thousand inhabitants (some have several million). Many places in the US called 'cities' would be called 'towns' in Britain.

the City the financial district of London: the British equivalent of Wall Street. The City is governed by the Lord Mayor – whose post is largely ceremonial, and quite separate from the Mayor of London (who is an elected official responsible for the entire metropolis of London).

city centre the central part of a city; the area known as 'downtown' or the 'central business district' in other English-speaking countries

close a street closed at one end, also called a **dead-end street**; also an enclosure or enclosed place, such as a precinct of a cathedral. Pronounced as in 'dose', not 'doze'. The word dates back to medieval England and originates from Old French *clos*.

common area of land, usually grassy, held in common ownership by all members of a community; sometimes the common may be owned by an individual but others in the community still have right of access

high street the primary street or road in a town, where the bulk of the shops are – the butcher, the baker, the greengrocer, the newsagent, the chemist and so on. It's not the exact equivalent of US 'main street', but it has a similar meaning.

market town in the medieval period, towns depended on trade to prosper and grow, but had to gain permission from the monarch, in the form of a royal charter, to hold regular markets. Those that did were designated market towns. Today it's a term for any medium-sized town, usually one that has existed for a few centuries at least.

DOWNTOWN & DOWN TOWN

When someone who lives in the countryside says they are going **down town** it means they are going into town. However, when someone who lives in the city says they are going **downtown**, it means they are going to the heart of the city where all the bars, restaurants and entertainment are concentrated.

the Met abbreviation for the London Metropolitan Police Department. (Not to be confused with the **Met Office**, which is short for the Meteorological Office – Britain's national weather service.)

mews dwellings grouped around an open yard or alley

minster alternative word for cathedral (as in York Minster). Hence Westminster – from West Minster – the original name of the great church built in the medieval period to the west of the original City of London, and now giving its name to the surrounding area.

pavement paved pedestrian walkway beside a road; 'sidewalk' in US English, 'footpath' in Australian English

village a rural settlement, usually of a few hundred inhabitants – smaller than a town. Some definitions state that a village must have a few facilities (such as a post office, pub, shop, church and primary school) but the term is used to mean 'any small settlement'. If a place is really small (just a few houses and maybe a church) it's called a **hamlet**.

Countrywise

Many countries are identified with a particular natural or manmade topographical feature – think of Russia's steppes, America's prairies or Holland's dykes and canals. Britain also has its special features; here's a small selection:

barrow prehistoric burial mound. Numerous **barrows** exist in Britain, many dating from the Bronze Age.

bridleway path originally for horse-riders, but which can also be used by walkers and cyclists

broad low-lying lake (in east England). **The Broads** is an area of wetlands in the county of Norfolk in eastern England.

dale valley, usually small or medium-sized, often in the chalk-land or limestone areas of northern England

downs treeless, grass-covered undulating hills, usually on chalk soil, especially in southern England; also called **downlands**. (No, you didn't misread – the downlands are uplands.)

"BRIDLEWAY – A PATH FOR HORSE RIDERS, WALKERS AND CYCLISTS"

fen low, marshy area of land. **The Fens** is a formerly marshy area of eastern England, now drained by a network of canals and ditches (many called **dykes**) and a rich farming area.

firth river estuary, such as the Firth of Forth and the Firth of Clyde in Scotland. The word is related to the Norse word *fjord*.

footpath path for walkers or hikers in a rural area, or a path in an urban area that doesn't run along the roadside. Many are **rights of way** – see the box on p65.

gorse bush with sharp thick spines and small yellow flowers that grows on heath and other sandy areas. Also known as **furze**.

heath tract of open land, generally covered with low, patchy shrubs such as **broom** or **gorse**; also called **heathland**

hedgerow very large hedge containing numerous different species of tree and bush, and forming a barrier around farmland – effectively a natural wall or fence

moor area of high open land with dark peaty soil, usually devoid of trees and covered in rough grass and plants such as heather. Emily Brontë's *Wuthering Heights* is set on the moors of West Yorkshire, near Haworth.

plantation in Britain, this is an area planted with trees, particularly conifers (rather than, say, bananas or cotton)

wold hill, as in the Yorkshire Wolds, Lincolnshire Wolds and the Cotswolds (which is where you find the **market town** of Stow-on-the-Wold)

Getting around

Behind the wheel

There are five main types of road in Britain. **Motorways** are the high-speed routes that go from city to city. In other English-speaking countries they are known as 'freeways' or 'interstates'. British motorways are identified by numbers, like the **M1** (London to Leeds). **A-roads** are the main highways after motorways, and then come **B-roads**, which are smaller, though often still quite busy. **C-roads** are more often called **lanes** or **country roads**, while **unclassified roads** are found in remote or rural areas and are still tarred, but often only wide enough for one car. Note that in Britain, the term **street** always means a road in a town or city.

Whether driving down the road or up the street, here are some British terms to do with motor vehicles and the places they go:

articulated lorry or **artic** large truck with a cab and separate trailer attached by a joint

bonnet the hinged panel at the front of the car, covering the engine. Called the 'hood' in the US.

boot the storage space at the back of the car, where you put your bags. The 'trunk' in the US.

caravan a 'house' on wheels, towed behind a car, usually for holiday purposes. Caravans are often called 'trailers' in

GO THE RIGHT WAY

Perhaps because Britain is such a crowded place, open spaces are highly valued, and every weekend millions of Britons get their boots on and take to the countryside. Every town and village is surrounded by a web of footpaths, while most patches of open land are crossed by paths and tracks.

The joy of walking in Britain is due in no small part to the **right of way** network – public paths and tracks across private property. Nearly all land in Britain is privately owned (including land within national parks), but if there's a right of way, you can follow it through fields, woods, even farmhouse yards, as long as you keep to the route and do no damage. Some mountain and moorland areas of England and Wales are **Open Access Areas**, where walkers can move freely beyond rights of way (signboards or maps indicate when this is permitted). Scotland has a different system, with fewer actual rights of way, but a tradition of relatively free access in mountain and moorland areas – although there are restrictions during the grouse- and deer-hunting seasons.

The main types of right of way are **footpaths** and **bridleways** (the latter open to horse-riders and mountain-bikers too). There are also **byways**, unsurfaced tracks which due to a quirk of history are open to all traffic. This means walkers can be disturbed by off-road driving fanatics – a cause of considerable controversy in some areas.

US English. In British English, very big caravans are called **mobile homes** – ironic since they're often so big they're not really mobile. These are also called **static caravans** or simply **statics**.

car park the place where you park your car, called a 'parking lot' in the US. A **multistorey car park** is what Americans might call a 'parking garage'.

THE NEED FOR SPEED

Most British drivers tend to **speed** (ie go faster than the legal limit). The presence of **speed traps** (police with radar guns) and **speed cameras** (automatic detection cameras, often called **Gatzos** – a brand name now used generically) doesn't have much impact. Even being stopped by the police and **done for speeding** (fined) doesn't seem to be a deterrent.

central reservation a length of concrete or grass dividing the traffic going in opposite directions on a multilane highway (nothing to do with an area for indigenous inhabitants). Called a 'median strip' in US and Australian English.

diversion detour (eg because the road is being repaired)

full beam see **high beam**

gearstick device for changing gears in a car – known to Americans as a 'gearshift' or 'stickshift'

handbrake what Americans call the 'emergency brake' or 'parking brake'

high beam headlights usually have two settings: high beam points straight ahead; **dipped** is when the light is dimmed to avoid dazzling on-coming drivers. The extra-strong headlights used on dark country roads at night or during bad weather at any time are called **foglights** or **spotlights**.

lay-by a parking place at the side of a main road, usually with no facilities other than an overflowing rubbish bin (compare with **services**)

lorry a large goods vehicle – usually called a 'truck' elsewhere, although that term is used in Britain too

pelican crossing road crossing with pedestrian-activated traffic lights. 'Pelican' is a tortured acronym of 'Pedestrian Light-Controlled'.

petrol fuel for cars; 'gasoline' in the US

services a place where you can turn off the motorway to stop, rest, put petrol in your car, and get something to eat (eg: 'I'm dying for the loo, how far is it to the next services?')

subway an underground pedestrian passage used to get from one side of a road to the other. Not a place where underground trains run, as in New York.

tarmac the term **tarmac road** is used to mean any road surfaced in asphalt (as opposed to concrete)

tyre British spelling of US 'tire'

verge the strip on the side of the road; called the 'shoulder' in US and Australian English

windscreen window at the front of a car; called a 'windshield' in the US

zebra crossing pedestrian road crossing, marked by black-and-white stripes painted on the road – hence the name

Ticket to ride

Britain's public transport systems of bus and train networks can be a great way to get around. Note that it's always called **public transport**, not 'public transportation' as in the US.

> "THE CHUNNEL – THE TUNNEL UNDER THE ENGLISH CHANNEL LINKING BRITAIN AND FRANCE"

The wheels on the bus

In Britain there's an important difference between a **bus**, which normally means a local bus, and a **coach**, which is normally a long-distance bus, often faster and more comfortable. In some towns and cities the **bus station** and the **coach station** are in different places, causing great confusion for visitors.

A few other terms:

bus shelter small building or some transparent plastic panels providing protection from the elements for passengers waiting at a **bus stop**

bus station large building or area where many buses pass through or start/terminate their route

bus stop a point on the road, usually marked by a sign, where a bus stops to pick up or set down passengers

double-decker bus with two floors

Routemaster the brand name of the original red London **double-decker** bus, regarded by many as an icon. The fleet was withdrawn in 2005 after many decades of service, and is now being replaced with the **New Bus for London** (**NBfL**), first introduced in 2012 and featuring not one but two staircases.

Let the train take the strain

There are two main sorts of train service on Britain's railways: **long-distance** or **inter-city** services; and **local** or **commuter** services. Here are some more rail-related terms:

booking office place to buy tickets – especially for travel at a later date

buffet a small café at a train station or on a train (where it's often called the **buffet car**)

Channel Tunnel the tunnel under the English Channel which links Britain with France, through which high-speed

HAIL, TAXI

Although the traditional **London cab** (also called **black cabs** or **black taxis**, despite the fact that they now come in a variety of colours) is not the cheapest way to get around London and other major cities, passengers can be sure of getting to their destination by the quickest possible route. To get a licence, London's **cabbies** (taxi drivers) must memorise thousands of streets, as well as the position of hotels, theatres, railway stations and a host of other locations. This font of expertise is known simply as **the Knowledge**.

Minicabs are freelance taxis that can only be hired by phone (not flagged down in the street), and are generally cheaper than black cabs. Drivers are not required to have the Knowledge, and passengers often find themselves having to give minicab drivers the most basic of directions.

trains carry passengers and vehicles. Occasionally dubbed the **Chunnel**.

level crossing point where a road crosses a railway line on the same level (ie not via a bridge). The crossing is usually protected by gates which close when a train passes.

Oyster card Oyster is a plastic smartcard you can use instead of paper tickets on the Underground, buses and trams in London. National Rail services within London also accept Oyster.

railway generic term for the rail network; 'railroad' in the US

return ticket a ticket which allows you to go to and come back from your destination

single ticket a ticket for a one-way journey

standard class the seating formerly known as 'second class'

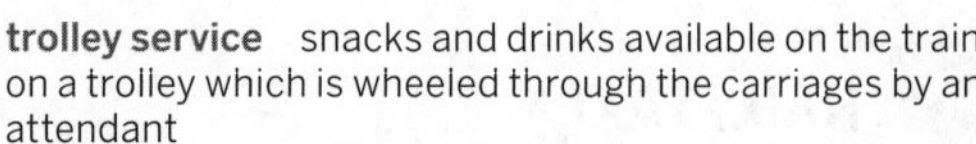

trolley service snacks and drinks available on the train on a trolley which is wheeled through the carriages by an attendant

the Tube colloquial name for London's underground railway network

way out exit

EATING, DRINKING & MAKING MERRY

CLASSIC PHRASE:

CHEERS!

The typical salutation when raising your glass

TRY THIS ONE:

'FANCY A CUPPA?'

A phrase that will endear you to any tea-loving Brit – 'cuppa' is the shortened version of 'cup of tea'

USE WITH CAUTION:

'I'LL HAVE A SNAKEBITE'

A notoriously effective mix of cider and lager – favoured by students for rapid and inexpensive inebriation

MISUNDERSTANDINGS:

'IT'S YOUR SHOUT'

Please don't yell! A shout is a round of drinks and this means it's your turn to buy them.

EATING, DRINKING & MAKING MERRY

Britain once had a cuisine so undesirable that it's no wonder there's no English equivalent of *Bon appétit*. Fortunately, these days it's easy to find decent food as Britain now boasts more than its fair share of Michelin-starred restaurants.

Having said that, Britain's culinary heritage still boasts treats like **pork scratchings** and **deep-fried Mars bars**. (The latter was invented in Glasgow, so perhaps it's no surprise that Scotland, with help from high cigarette and alcohol consumption, has one of the worst rates of heart disease in Europe.)

The recent changes for the better in food in Britain are largely thanks to outside influences. Chinese and Indian restaurants have been around since the 1960s and are no longer considered exotic. In fact, curry is the most popular takeaway food in Britain, outstripping even fish and chips.

In more recent times Britain has seen the arrival of restaurants specialising in food from the Mediterranean region, Africa, the Caribbean, Japan, Thailand, Vietnam and many other countries. As a result, pastas, pizzas, tapas, moussaka, sushi, foo yung, baklava and other specialities are commonplace in restaurants, and even in everyday pubs and cafés.

> "NOSH
> — FOOD"

FISH & CHIPS

Served in pubs and cafés, or available from takeaway shops (often known as **chippies**), fish and chips is a popular meal across Britain. Sometimes both the chips and the fish can be greasy and tasteless (especially once you get far from the sea), but good chips seem to go with good fish, so at towns with salt in the air this deep-fried delight is always worth trying.

The overall effect of these foreign influences has been the introduction of revolutionary ingredients, new condiments, new techniques and new implements to restaurants and kitchens across Britain. In the smarter eating houses, a mix of British food with cuisine from anywhere else is known as **fusion cooking**. In more modest environments, such as country pubs in the north of England, look out for crossover dishes like **Yorkshire pudding** filled with curry – a favourite that many would say epitomises British society today.

Grub's up

Options for eating out in Britain are many and varied, but a good start is always a local **café** (usually pronounced 'caffy' and often shortened to **caff**). A British café can be a **greasy spoon** (a very straightforward snack bar where cleanliness isn't always top priority), or a smart and welcoming place with luxuries like napkins and tablecloths (sometimes called a **teashop**) – or it can be something in between.

Either way, a British café is not the same as a café in France. For a start, asking for Pernod may cause confusion, as most British cafés don't serve alcohol.

Here are some other terms the Brits use when dining out:

bill payment at a restaurant, at the end of the meal. You can ask for the bill, but not the 'check'. In Britain, a **cheque** is used to pay for goods or services, instead of using cash or a credit card; it's the thing you tear out of your **chequebook**.

canteen in British English this is a snack bar or refreshment room, usually found in places like factories, offices, schools, hospitals and military camps

dinner a main meal. Depending on where you are in Britain, this can mean the main meal around midday or the main meal in the evening (see the box below).

tea as well as the drink, tea can mean a meal in the evening. It can also mean a midafternoon meal consisting of cakes, sandwiches or scones, served of course with a cup of tea. The term **high tea** is sometimes used for the latter variety, to distinguish it from 'normal' tea.

ARE WE EATING LUNCH OR DINNER?

In different areas of Britain, the term **dinner** can be used differently. In the south of England (and at any restaurant) it's a cooked evening meal. But in northern England it's the meal eaten around noon. Thus, factory workers in the south have a **lunch break**, while those in the north have a **dinner break**. The difference isn't always regional; it can be more of a class divide too – the posh folks say 'lunch', while the workers say 'dinner'.

The term **tea** is similarly divided. In the south it means a light meal or snack midafternoon. In the north, where dinner is eaten at noon, tea is the cooked meal in the evening.

If you happen to be making arrangements to meet someone in Britain, and they say 'Come round after dinner', it might be worth checking if this means 2pm or 8pm...

Bacon & bangers for brekkie

There are many ingredients and dishes unique to Britain, and even for the most globally recognisable items, visitors may have to deal with unusual names. A few are listed below.

Many of these words will be recognised by speakers of Australian, Canadian and New Zealand English (which share many similarities with modern British English), but may be more unusual to speakers of American English.

bacon in Britain this means a cut of pork, generally taken from the back of the pig, cured, smoked or salted, and thinly sliced. It's most commonly fried or grilled and eaten for breakfast or in a sandwich. It's often called 'Canadian bacon' in America.

bangers colloquial term for sausages, often eaten with **mash** (mashed potato)

bannock Scottish speciality – a cross between a scone and a pancake

bap a large, wide, flat, soft bread roll

bara brith traditional Welsh spicy fruit loaf

biscuits this generally means sweet biscuits ('cookies' in the US). The terms **savoury biscuits**, **salted biscuits** or

HAM IT UP

In some parts of Britain, bacon is called **ham**, and so **cooked ham** describes the stuff you can eat straight away, as opposed to the stuff you have to grill or fry before slapping between two bits of bread.

NAME THAT PASTY

The **Cornish pasty** – a mix of cooked meat and vegetables wrapped in pastry – is now available everywhere in Britain, not just Cornwall. However, having been granted Protected Geographical Indication (PGI) status in 2011, the term 'Cornish pasty' can now only be applied to pasties that are prepared in Cornwall and contain set ingredients.

Long before Tupperware, the **pasty** was an all-in-one lunch pack that tin miners could carry underground and leave on a ledge ready for mealtime. To avoid mixing pasties, each was marked with the owner's initials – always at one end, so the miner could eat half and leave the rest to snack on later without it mistakenly being eaten by a workmate.

Before going back to the surface, the miners traditionally left the last corner of the pasty as a gift for the spirits of the mine known as **knockers**, to ensure a safe shift next day.

cheese biscuits are usually used for what Americans call 'crackers' (though the words **crackers** or **cream crackers** are also sometimes used in Britain).

bun bread roll, usually sweet – eg **currant bun**, **cream bun**

cawl (pronounced 'cow') traditional Welsh dish; a thick broth of mixed vegetables, or vegetables and meat

chips hot deep-fried potato pieces (called 'french fries' or 'fries' in the US) and traditionally eaten with fish

clotted cream cream so heavy or rich that it's become almost solid (but not sour)

courgette (pronounced 'cawzhet' – the *g* is pronounced like the *s* in 'measure') the French word is used for this long thin green member of the gourd family. Called 'zucchini' in the US and Australia.

"SPOTTED DICK
– A CLASSIC ENGLISH DESSERT"

cream cracker white unsalted savoury biscuit

cream tea a special **tea** or **high tea** (see p75) of **scones**, **clotted cream** and **jam**, served with a cup or pot of tea. This is known as a **Devonshire tea** in many English-speaking countries, but not in England (except of course in the county of Devon).

crisps thin slices of fried potato bought in a packet. Called 'potato chips', or just 'chips' in the US and Australia.

crumpet circular kind of bread, one side covered in small indentations, which is toasted and usually buttered lavishly before being eaten

Dundee cake fruit cake made with a particularly rich fruit mix and topped with almonds – a Scottish speciality but widely available in Britain

fishfinger strip of fish pieces covered in breadcrumbs, usually bought frozen and cooked by frying or grilling – a children's favourite

gammon thick slice of ham, in the sense of a 'ham steak' on a dinner menu, rather than a thin slice of breakfast ham (which is called **bacon** in most parts of Britain)

haggis traditional Scottish dish of ground meat or offal mixed with oatmeal, stuffed in a sheep's stomach or intestine, then baked. Originally a poor-man's sausage, it's now regarded as a delicacy in some areas. Some pubs and restaurants in Scotland serve very good haggis; it's also available deep-fried with **chips** at takeaways.

ice lolly in Britain this is flavoured ice on a stick

jam fruit conserve. In US English 'jam' contains pieces of fruit, while 'jelly' has been strained. This distinction exists in British English, but the term jam is often used for the strained stuff as well.

jelly gelatine dessert, often poured into a mould to set; called 'Jell-O' in US English

kipper smoked herring

laverbread a Welsh speciality that's not a bread at all, but cooked seaweed. It's traditionally served mixed up with oatmeal and bacon on toast – a very tasty combination.

lollipop/lollypop/lolly a **sweet** on a stick. If it's not on a stick, it's not a lolly (unlike in Australia). See the box on p80 for more.

Marmite a dark and pungent yeast extract, usually spread on toast, that generations of Brits have either loved or hated from childhood. Similar to the Aussie favourite Vegemite, but not the same – oh no!

munchies a slang term used to mean 'hungry' (as in 'I've got the munchies'). It's especially used in the context of the deep desire for food resulting from serious drinking or the use of some recreational drugs – notably cannabis.

nosh food

pasty (pronounced 'pastee' with an *a* as in 'apple') a half-moon-shaped savoury pastry, crimped along the curved side and filled with meat or vegetables. Its most famous form is the **Cornish pasty**.

pickle a thick, vinegary vegetable-based condiment. Called 'relish' in US English.

ploughman's lunch thick slices of bread and cheese, commonly served in pubs, now available in many varieties

pork scratchings deep-fried chunks of pig skin and fat, often sold in packets in pubs. Heavy in calories, and an acquired taste.

porridge called 'oatmeal' by North Americans

pudding this can mean a sweet dessert such as **butterscotch** or **chocolate pudding**, or a type of cake

SUCK IT AND SEE

In Britain, **sweets** (young children might say **sweeties**) are the equivalent of what Americans call 'candy', and what the Americans call a 'candy bar' is usually called a **bar of chocolate** in Britain. If you want to buy a 'sucker', you'll have to ask for a **lollipop** or a **lolly**. And Australians, note that for the Brits a lolly is a sweet on a stick – not any sweet at all.

(eg **Bakewell pudding**), or a savoury dish (like **steak and kidney pudding**). It's also a general word for 'dessert'.

scone a small doughy bread, traditionally served with jam and cream. Pronounced either 'scon' (to rhyme with 'on') or 'scown' (to rhyme with 'own').

shepherd's pie a two-layered oven dish with a ground beef and onion mixture on the bottom and mashed potato on the top. Though it's called a pie, there's no crust.

spotted dick this sounds like an embarrassing disease, but it's really a dessert – suet pudding with currants and raisins

treacle molasses or dark syrup

trifle dessert made from a mixture of sponge cake, whipped cream, custard, **jelly**, fruit and sherry or spirits

Welsh rarebit a sophisticated variation of cheese on toast, in which the cheese is seasoned and flavoured with butter, milk and sometimes a little beer. Originally called Welsh rabbit. (Maybe a modern Trades Description law forced the name change?)

Worcestershire sauce a condiment made from anchovies, chillies, garlic and molasses, among other things, introduced to Britain from Bengal during Victorian times. Although the county **Worcestershire** is pronounced 'woostersheer', this sauce is always called just 'wooster'.

Let's have a bevvy

In Britain a **drink** means any ingestible liquid, so if a British person asks if you'd like a drink, don't automatically expect a beer or a whisky. They may well be offering a **cuppa** – a cup of tea – the British national drink.

Nonalcoholic drinks

Following are some terms used to describe nonalcoholic drinks:

cordial	sweetened fruit drink
lemonade	lemon-flavoured carbonated soft drink. Only the term **handmade lemonade** means freshly squeezed lemon juice, water and sugar.
pop	any carbonated soft drink
squash	fruit drink concentrate mixed with water
White or black?	the British way of asking if you'd like milk in your tea or coffee

Alcoholic drinks

A lot of beer and wine in Britain is bought at a supermarket or **off-licence** (a shop selling alcohol to be consumed elsewhere – it might be called a 'liquor store' or 'bottle shop' in other countries). However, large quantities are also consumed at the **pub** – short for 'public house' – the common term for Britain's traditional drinking establishment. (More modern places are called a **bar**, rather than a pub.)

People generally have a favourite pub near their home that they call their **local**. In villages, towns and city suburbs it's a place for neighbours to gather and chat, making the pub effectively an informal meeting room at the heart of the community.

Inner-city pubs can have a different feel from their country or suburban cousins, however. They're often busier, with less of a local feel – but often still a perfect place for a **pint**.

Here are some terms used by British **tipplers**:

ale typical British beer is technically called ale, but in practice is more commonly called **bitter**. It's dark brown in colour and generally served at room temperature. Ale should not be confused with **lager**.

bevvy (slang) an alcoholic drink; hence **bevvying** means 'drinking'. The word can also be used to imply an evening of drinking, as in 'Are you coming for a bevvy tonight?'

bitter generally used as a synonym for **ale**, as opposed to **lager**

BYO on a restaurant sign, an indication that you can **Bring Your Own** alcoholic drinks to a restaurant – usually one that doesn't have a licence to sell these drinks

cider alcoholic drink made from apples, similar in strength to beer (not a spirit)

corkage the fee charged by restaurants for the **BYO** wines you brought

double in British pubs, spirits are served in measures called **singles** and **doubles**. A **single** is 35ml – just over one US fluid ounce. A **double** is of course 70ml – still disappointingly small when compared to measures in other countries!

CHEERS, M'DEARS

Cheers is the usual salutation when raising a glass. But in other circumstances it also means 'thanks' or 'goodbye'. As with so many words in British English, context is everything.

KEEP IT REAL

A nice cup of tea might be the favourite British drink, but a nice pint of beer isn't far behind. For some visitors to Britain, a traditional **bitter** (also known as **real ale**) may come as a shock – a warm, flat and expensive shock. This is partly to do with Britain's climate (it's not hot, so beer doesn't need to be cold), and partly with the beer being served by hand-pump rather than gas-pressure.

Most important, though, is the integral flavour: traditional British beer doesn't need to be chilled or fizzed. Another key feature of real ale is that it must be stored and served with care (that's why many pubs don't serve it). Beware of places that give the barrels as much care as the condom machine in the toilets. There's nothing worse than a bad pint of real ale – you might as well have a bottle of cheap lager.

free house a pub that doesn't belong to a brewery or pub company, thus is 'free' to sell any brewer's beer. Unfortunately, it doesn't mean the beer is free of charge. The opposite is a **tied house**.

lager a beer that's generally yellow in colour and served cold (eg Foster's or Carling), unlike **ale**

lager top lager with a dash of lemonade. You can also get a **cider top** or a **bitter top**.

local the neighbourhood or village pub. **Going down the local** is a great British pastime.

neat referring to how a drink is taken, and meaning not mixed with water or a soft drink. Equivalent terms include **straight** (but not 'straight up' in British English – that means 'honestly').

off-licence a shop licensed to sell alcohol to 'be consumed off the premises'; ie to take away. Shortened to **offie** or **beer-off** in some parts of Britain.

ONE FOR YOURSELF

In British pubs, drinks are ordered and paid for at the bar, and it's not usual to tip the bar staff (unlike in America). However, if you're ordering a large round, or the service has been good all evening, you can say to the person behind the bar **...and one for yourself**. They will add the cost of a drink to your bill – and either keep the money as a tip, or use it to buy a drink later when they're off duty.

round several drinks bought at the same time, generally for a group of friends. It's usually reciprocal. If someone says **It's your round**, **It's your shout** or **Go and get a round in**, they mean that it's your turn to buy everyone in the group a drink. An impoverished friend might say 'Sorry, guys, I can't get in a round. I've only got a couple of quid on me, so I'll have to buy me own'.

scrumpy a type of strong dry **cider** originally made in England's West Country. Many pubs serve it straight from the barrel.

shout a colloquial term meaning 'to buy a drink or drinks for others'. **My shout** means 'I'll pay'. If someone says **It's your shout**, they mean 'It's your turn to buy'.

snakebite an equal mix of **cider** and **lager**. Favoured by students, as it reputedly gets you drunk quickly and cheaply – thanks to the lager's bubbles and the cider's strength.

snug from a word meaning 'warm', this is usually a small separate room in a pub, or sometimes an enclosed part of a larger room. Traditionally, snugs have a coal fire.

"BEVVY, TIPPLE
— ALCOHOLIC DRINK"

stout a dark, full-bodied beer made from malt. Guinness is the most famous variety.

tied house a pub which is limited to selling the products of one particular brewery, thus making it 'tied' to that brewer. The opposite is a **free house**.

tipple an old-fashioned word for a drink ('Do you fancy a tipple?'). A **tippler** is a drinker.

Drunk again...

Believe it or not, all the expressions below are slang words or regional terms for being drunk.

arseholed, battered, bevvied, bevvied up, bladdered, blootered, bollocksed, bricked, buckled, buttwhipped, cabbaged, canned, creamed, crushed, cunted, floored, foetal, fucked, guttered, hammered, hamstered, kalied, kaly, lashed, leathered, leery, legless, mashed, monged, mortal, mortalled, off it,

WATER OF LIFE

The word **whisky** (always spelt without an *e* in Britain, when describing Scotland's most famous export) is derived from the Scottish Gaelic **uisge beatha** – pronounced *oosh*·kuh *beh*·huh – which literally means 'water of life'.

The two main kinds of whisky are **single malt whisky**, made from malted barley; and **blended whisky**, made from unmalted grain which is then blended with one or more malt whiskies. The quality of blended whisky can vary. Single malts are usually better quality, rarer (there are only about 100 brands) and more expensive.

When ordering a **dram** (a drink of whisky) in Scotland, remember to ask for whisky – only the English and other foreigners say 'Scotch'. What else would you be served in Scotland?

off my face, off my trolley, out of my face, out of my head, out of my tree, palatic, para, paralytic, pished, pissed, pissed as a fart, pissed as a newt, pissed up, plonked, rat-arsed, ratted, reeling, scoobied, shedded, shitfaced, slashed, slaughtered, slewed, sloshed, sozzled, steaming, stotted, tanked, tankered, tired and emotional, trashed, trolleyed, twatted, wankered, wasted, wazzed, well gone, wellied, wrecked

And while we're on the subject, here are some choice expressions for vomit or vomiting:

barf, blow, blow chunks, blow your groceries, boak, chak, chuck, chunder, flurg, heave, hurl, lose your lunch, pavement pizza, praying to the porcelain god, razz, retch, shouting down the big white telephone, spew, technicolour yawn, throw, throw up, vom, yak

Isn't British English a delightful language? These words just roll off the tongue, don't they? Rather like the experience they describe...

SPORT & ENTERTAINMENT

Look out for these...

CLASSIC PHRASE:

PUNTERS

Commonly used term for customers - not just at the race track

TRY THIS ONE:

P'S AND QUIDS

It's all about money: A pee is a penny and a quid is a pound

USE WITH CAUTION:

BOOB TUBE

While this is slang for a television set in America, in Britain it means a tight-fitting strapless top.

MISUNDERSTANDINGS:

HAVING IT LARGE

Not super-sizing, but having a big night out

SPORT

If you want to take a shortcut into the heart of British culture, watch the British at play. They're fierce and passionate about their sport, whether participating or watching. The mood of the nation is more closely aligned to the success of its international teams than to even the weather forecasts.

Britain gave the world many of its most popular sports, including football, rugby and golf - and then the world started beating the creators at their own games. But that doesn't dampen British enthusiasm. There's always a major sporting event happening somewhere that preoccupies the nation.

Football

Some people may know this game as 'soccer', but in Britain it's definitely called football, and it's by far the most popular sport in the country.

It's been played for many centuries, although it's unclear exactly when an inter-village competition involving two unruly mobs kicking around a pig's bladder developed into the 'beautiful game'. Scholars put it sometime in the 12th century.

In the following 800 years, and despite repeated royal bans, the game grew in popularity. In the 19th century, the Football Association was founded and the formal rules of the game as we know it today were laid down.

A league of their own

The English League comprises four divisions. At the zenith is the elite Premier League, for the country's top 20 clubs - including globally renowned Manchester United, Chelsea, Arsenal and Liverpool. Beneath the Premier League are the Championship, League One and League Two.

The system works on the principles of promotion and relegation, so after each season (from August to May) the teams that finish near the bottom of each league get relegated to the next division down, and the teams that finish near the top of the lower division get promoted to the next level up.

Scotland has a separate (though smaller) league structured in the same way as England's. The teams from England and Scotland don't play any domestic games against one another but occasionally meet in European competition.

In Wales, football is less popular, although some of the bigger teams play in the English League.

How it works

Disregarding the notorious **offside** rule (which nearly every newcomer to the game has difficulty grasping), football is remarkably straightforward. The aim of each team is to score a **goal** by kicking the round-shaped ball between the posts and under the crossbar of the opposition's goal, while at the same time defending their own goal.

SOCK IT TO ME

Football is officially called **association football**, to distinguish it from **rugby football** – the official name for rugby – as well as from Gaelic football, American football, Australian Rules football, and other variations. The word 'soccer' (the favoured term in countries where football means another game) is reputedly an abbreviation of 'Association'; although another theory holds that it's derived from the term 'sock'. In Medieval times a 'sock' was a tough leather foot-covering, worn especially by peasants – just the types who'd enjoy kicking around a pig's bladder with a bunch of mates on a Saturday afternoon.

BE A SPORT

Generally speaking, the Brits refer to **sport** in the singular. For example, a fan might say: 'I love sport, me. Football, cricket, horseracing – all of them.'

Players are allowed to use any part of their body except their hands and arms to block or control the ball, but only the feet and head may be used for striking it.

There are 11 players on each team and five **substitutes** (usually called **subs**) **on the bench** (ie at the side of the pitch) ready to join the game at a moment's notice if another player is injured or called off by the manager. Up to three subs can be used during a game to replace any of the original 11.

Matches have two 45-minute halves with a 15-minute interval in between. Although football is a contact sport, players aren't allowed to grab, tug, strike or kick opponents, or push them with their hands. Firm use of the shoulders when players are running for the ball is allowed, however.

Football is a very low-scoring game compared to most team sports – the lack of goals may be one of the reasons football isn't so popular in the US or Australia. No-score draws are reasonably common, but for fans this doesn't mean football isn't entertaining. It's the quality of the play, the tension, the chances and the near misses that make the game – although a goal or two (for the side you support) always puts the icing on the cake.

The positions

The players in each team fall into three main types: **attackers** (or **strikers**), **defenders** and **midfielders** (who act as a link between the attackers and defenders and are also often involved in attack and defence themselves). The **goalkeeper** (often shortened to goalie or keeper) is confined to the goal area. Teams play various formations to get the best result out of each game. A standard formation is 4-4-2, which means there are four defenders, four midfielders and two strikers. A more attacking formation would be 3-5-2, where the team decides to play only three defenders and an extra midfielder in order to put more pressure on the opposition's goal.

> "WAGS – THE WIVES AND GIRLFRIENDS OF STAR FOOTBALLERS"

Match of the day

Each football season kicks off with the Charity Shield – a match between the winners of the previous year's Premier League and FA Cup competitions. The season climaxes in May each year with the FA Cup Final – traditionally held at Wembley Stadium in North London, but with a few years out at Cardiff's Millennium Stadium while Wembley was being rebuilt.

Some British football terms you might hear include:

booking a warning to a player from the referee, usually after committing a foul (breaking a rule of the game)

cross this means kicking the ball across the pitch, instead of up or down. It's often used when the ball is kicked across the face of the goal in an attempt to score.

half-time the break halfway through the game

header when a player strikes the ball with the head, rather than the foot

kick-off the start of the game

offside an attacking player can't be passed the ball by another player on the same team if there's no player from the opposing team between them and the goal. If this happens, the attacking player receiving the ball is offside. A strategy often employed by defending players is to move forward (ie away from their goal) so that a player from the attacking side suddenly finds themselves in an **offside position**, and unable to receive the ball. The rule was developed to prevent **goal-hanging** (waiting very close to the goal).

penalty a free shot at the goal awarded when a defending player fouls an attacking opponent in the area in front of the goal (called the **penalty box**). Penalties are taken from the **penalty spot**.

red card a player committing a serious foul is **booked** then shown a **yellow card** by the referee. A player getting two yellow cards in the same game is then shown a red card and expelled from the game. If the foul is serious

THE FA CUP

The Football Association held its first interclub knockout tournament in 1871. Fifteen clubs took part, playing for a nice piece of silverware called the FA Cup – then worth about £20. Nowadays, around 600 clubs compete for this legendary and priceless trophy. It differs from many other competitions in that every team – from the lowest-ranking part-timers to the stars of the Premier League – is in with a chance. Public attention is invariably focused on the **giant-killers** – minor clubs that claw their way up through the rounds, unexpectedly beating higher-ranking competitors. One of the best-known giant-killing events occurred in 1992, when Wrexham, then ranked 24th in Division 3, famously beat league champions Arsenal.

enough, the player may be shown the red card without an initial warning.

referee's assistant proper name for an official who monitors the game from the side of the pitch – there are two at most matches. The common name for this official is a **linesman**.

skipper a colloquial term for the team captain, who normally wears an armband to indicate captaincy

sweeper a defensive position – a player who 'sweeps away' the ball if it's passed towards the goal

yellow card see **red card**

WAG the wife or girlfriend of a footballer

Cricket

The quintessentially English game of **cricket** (it's far more popular in England than in Wales or Scotland) has been played formally since the 18th century – although its roots go much further back. Cricket became an international game during Britain's colonial era, when it was exported to the countries of the Commonwealth, particularly the Indian subcontinent, the West Indies and Australasia.

SPORTING GENTLEMEN

A wit once said that football is a gentleman's game played by hooligans, while rugby is a hooligan's game played by gentlemen. (Irish or Gaelic football, incidentally, is said to be a hooligan's game played by hooligans.)

Howzat!

A cricket team comprises 11 players. For each innings (a team's chance at batting), one team bats and the opposing team bowls. The bowling team has all its players on the field: one bowler and 10 fielders. The batting team is represented by two batsmen on the pitch. The other nine players sit in the pavilion waiting for their turn.

> "THE ASHES
> — SERIES OF TEST MATCHES BETWEEN AUSTRALIA AND ENGLAND"

The two batsmen each stand in front of a set of wickets (three wooden uprights called stumps, across which are balanced two smaller wooden cylinders called bails) spaced 22 yards apart on the pitch (a rectangle of very short grass in the middle of the circular or oval field). The bowler's aim is to get the batsman out. The batting team's aim is to score runs (points) by hitting the ball as far as possible and running up and down between the wickets. If the batsman does hit the ball, it's the aim of the fielders to catch it before it hits the ground.

The bowler must bowl the ball with a straight arm (if the arm is bent it's a throw, and against the rules), and is allowed six attempts (called an over). The batsmen don't have to attempt to hit each ball bowled to them. Neither do they have to run each time a ball is struck. After these six attempts, the over is over (are you keeping up?), and another bowler has another six attempts, bowling at the wicket at the opposite end of the pitch.

The bowler tries to get the batsman out or dismissed in two main ways: either by hitting the wicket with the ball or

by forcing the batsman to strike the ball into the air so that a fielder can catch it before it hits the ground. A third way a batsman can be ruled out is if the ball would have hit the wicket, but the batman's body blocks it. In this case the umpire can rule **leg before wicket** (usually shortened to **lbw**).

Also, if the batsmen are running and one of the fielders hits the wickets with the ball and dislodges a bail, then the nearest batsman is **run out** (often simply called **out**), giving rise to cries from the other players of **Howzat!** ('How was that?') to the umpire - this is known as **appealing**. (In total, there are 10 ways a batsman can get out, six of which happen fairly regularly, but these are the four main ones.)

When one batsman is out, he's replaced by a new one. The innings is over when 10 of the 11 in the team are out.

If the batsman strikes the ball and it reaches the **boundary** (the perimeter of the field of play), he's awarded four runs without the bother of actually having to do any running. If the ball goes over the boundary without bouncing first, he's awarded six runs.

ASHES TO ASHES

The result of a Test series between England and Australia is referred to as winning or losing **the Ashes**. This name derives from a mock obituary for English cricket printed in *The Times* newspaper in 1882, following an Australian victory. Until this year, England had dominated the international game. The obituary said that the 'body' (ie of English cricket) was cremated and the ashes taken to Australia. The name stuck, and England and Australia play against one another every two years, alternately in each country, both sides grimly determined to retain, or win, the Ashes.

> " HOWZAT!
> – AN APPEAL TO THE UMPIRE "

The competitions

The teams that make up the main domestic competition are drawn from the English counties and this level of competition is known as County Cricket.

The English national cricket team is known as the MCC, from Marylebone Cricket Club, and the home of English cricket (indeed of world cricket, many would say) is Lord's Cricket Ground in London.

International cricket matches are called Tests. The English team tours each year and hosts at least one tour from one of the other major cricket-playing nations (Australia, India, Pakistan, Sri Lanka, South Africa and the West Indies). The most important of these for English cricket fans is the series of Test matches against Australia, known as the Ashes (see the box opposite).

In Test matches, each team gets two innings and the game can last for five days. Even then, these matches often end in a draw because neither team has time to force a win. If this is your experience after watching your first five-day Test you'll (a) be unlucky and (b) probably never want to watch cricket again.

Other formats of cricket include one-day cricket (which lasts for one day, strangely enough) and Twenty20 cricket (where each team faces just 20 overs).

Rugby union

There are two codes of rugby played in Britain - rugby union and rugby league. **Rugby union** in England is traditionally the game of the middle and upper classes, and at Britain's top schools it is sometimes known as **rugger**.

Rugby union is played more in southern England, Wales and Scotland, while **rugby league** is traditionally played and supported by the working classes, and is played predominantly in northern England - although there's a lot of crossover.

Rugby traces its roots to a football match in 1823 at Rugby School, in Warwickshire, a county in central England. A player called William Ellis, frustrated at the limitations of mere kicking, reputedly picked up the ball and ran with it towards the opponents' goal. True to the sense of British fair play, rather than Ellis being dismissed from the game, a whole new sport was developed around his tactic. The Rugby Football Union (**RFU**) was formally inaugurated nearly 50 years later, in 1871.

BALLS?

Britain's major ball sports – football, cricket, rugby league and rugby union – are predominantly played by men, as indicated by terms such as 'batsman' (and the use of 'he' and 'him' throughout this Sport section). However, all these games are played by women too – with the women's national football, rugby and cricket teams often enjoying greater (though less publicised) success on the international field than their male counterparts.

Scrum down!

There are 15 players in each rugby union team. The aim is to carry the oval-shaped ball across the opponents' goal line and touch the ground. The player's hand must be on the ball as it's pressed down. This is called a **try** and is worth five points. After each try, the scoring team is awarded an opportunity to kick at the H-shaped goal posts. If the ball is successfully kicked between the posts and above the crossbar, a **goal** (also called a **conversion**) is scored and the team is awarded two points. When a goal is scored at any other time in the match by a player kicking the ball, either during play (called a **drop goal** or **field goal**) or when play has been halted because the other side committed an offence (called a **penalty**), it's worth three points.

Rugby is definitely a contact sport: **tackling** (grabbing or stalling) an opposing player is only prohibited above the shoulders - anywhere else on the body is allowed.

The players move the ball forward by carrying it, either running alone or in a **ruck** (see the definition on p100). The ball can also be thrown by hand from one player to another, but not forwards. When a player either deliberately or inadvertently moves the ball forward with his hands, it's called a **knock-on**, and a free ball is awarded to the other team.

The ball may be kicked forward from one player to another, as long as the receiving player was behind the kicking player when the ball was kicked - this is called **running onto the ball**

> "RUGGER
> — RUGBY UNION"

Beating the auld enemy

The most important annual competition for Britain's rugby union fans is the Six Nations Championship, held from February to March and contested by England, Scotland (Scotland know England as 'the auld enemy'), Wales, Italy, France and Ireland. (Ireland's team represents both the Republic and Northern Ireland.) Each team plays alternate home and away matches, and plays each of the other teams only once during the competition.

Within the Six Nations Championship are unofficial awards: if one team from the British Isles (England, Scotland, Wales and Ireland) beats all the others it wins the Triple Crown. If any team in the tournament beats all the others, it gets the Grand Slam. The last-placed team gets the dreaded Wooden Spoon.

England's home ground is Twickenham (known fondly as Twickers) in London. Scotland plays at Murrayfield in Edinburgh, and Wales plays at the Millennium Stadium in Cardiff. Some other rugby terms:

ruck when one or more players from each team are on their feet and in physical contact, supporting a player who's holding the ball, it's called a ruck (which in Britain is also a general slang term for a fight). The players help each other push against their opponents in an attempt to gain ground.

scrum originally a scrum was a disorderly struggle in which each team tried to force the ball and opposing players towards the opposing goal. Today it's an aspect of the game used to accomplish the same thing, but it only happens following an infringement or a breakdown in play. In rugby union, a scrum involves eight players from each side. The forwards from each team lock arms and put their heads down. The middle player in each front row is called the hooker and the players on either side of him are the props. The one at the back is called the Number 8. The scrum half puts the ball into the heart of the scrum when he thinks his team has the momentum and then races around behind his team-mates to gather the ball when they back-heel it out of the scrum, so that play can continue. That's the theory. In reality it often ends in a great pile-up.

Rugby league

Rugby league broke away from rugby union in England in the 1890s, when many of the rules changed and it rapidly became professional or semiprofessional at the top level. (Rugby union remained ostensibly amateur until the 1990s.)

Up & under!

Many of the rules and tactics in rugby league are similar to those in rugby union, although a major difference is that there are only 13 players in each team. A game consists of two 40-minute halves, with a 10-minute interval.

Players attempt to get the oval ball past their opponents by hand-passing (always backwards) or kicking (usually forwards, but the receiver must have run from behind the kicker).

THE OXFORD & CAMBRIDGE BOAT RACE

This famous rowing race between teams of eight from the two oldest universities in England takes place annually in late March or early April. The race dates from 1829 and is billed as the world's longest surviving sporting rivalry. The race distance is 6800m – three times the Olympic distance – and has never been cancelled due to bad weather, despite treacherous conditions which have caused boats to sink in the past.

If an attacking player carrying the ball is tackled and brought to the ground by the opposition, play pauses but (unlike in rugby union) the ball is retained by the attacking side. The defending team moves back, the tackled player regains his feet, heels the ball backwards to a team-mate, and the attack recommences. After six tackles, the other team gets possession of the ball, and their opportunity to score.

Grounding the ball beyond the opponent's goal line is called a **try**, which is worth four points. A try can be **converted** into a **goal** by kicking the ball over the crossbar and between the posts of the H-shaped goal (in the same way as in rugby union), for two points. Teams can also score a goal by kicking the ball during play (called a **drop goal**) for one point. A **penalty** goal is worth two points.

Other sports, games & hobbies

Bowls

Officially known as **lawn bowls**, this is a very old game with a reputation for attracting very old players. It's played with balls called **woods** that have one side weighted (the **bias**) so they run in a curved course. The game is traditionally played outdoors on a **green** (meaning a finely mown grass lawn - sometimes slightly domed, in which case the game is called **crown green bowling**), but there are also indoor tournaments. The players roll their woods at a smaller white ball (the **jack**), trying to get as close to it as possible. And that's it. Sounds simple but it's not. Perhaps only those mature in years have the patience to master the game.

Darts

Darts is primarily a pub game, popular throughout Britain, and many people play in local pub or club teams. But major competitions attract a huge following, and to replicate the atmosphere entire indoor arenas are turned into bars.

The rules are simple: players throw three darts consecutively at a circular board, which is divided up into sections with different numerical values from 1 to 20, plus a small circle in the middle of the dart board called the bullseye – worth 50 points. Each section is subdivided, with a small double area (so a player hitting the double 20 will score 40 points) and an even smaller treble area. Skilled players aim consistently for the treble 20, and if they strike it with all three darts they score 180. At the big games, this results in a drawn-out 'Oner-huuunderrred-and-eighteeee!' shout from the compere, much cheering from the audience, and vast amounts of alcohol being quaffed in celebration.

A player starts with 501 points, and the player's score is deducted from this until he or she reaches zero. Players must finish by hitting a double – for example, if there's 36 left to score, they must aim for double 18.

> "GREEN
> – WHERE BOWLS IS PLAYED"

Skittles

Skittles is a traditional pub game (played inside or out) in which players roll wooden balls at nine roughly cylindrical wooden blocks arranged in a diamond pattern. It's also called ninepins, and is similar in principle to the game called tenpin bowling. Until the 1980s many pubs had a skittle alley, but these days most have fallen into disuse and been turned into extra drinking areas.

There's also a more compact version of this game, called **table skittles**, where the ball is swung on a string.

> " Pot
> – GET A SNOOKER BALL IN THE POCKET "

Snooker

Snooker is a game related to pool, but requiring far more skill (say its proponents), and involving a table about four times the size of a pool table. Players use **cues** to strike balls, aiming to **pot** them (get them in pockets). There are 15 red balls and six balls of other colours - yellow, green, brown, blue, pink and black. Each time a red ball is potted, one point is scored and the player gets the opportunity to **pot a colour**. The coloured balls are worth more: two points for the least, yellow, ascending to seven points for the black. The red stays in the pocket after it's potted, but the colours are replaced in their original positions. Once all the reds are potted, the colours must be potted in the order given above.

ENTERTAINMENT

Since the dawn of the swinging '60s, Britain has been firmly on the main stage of pop and rock music. There's a thriving cinema industry too, although it's often overshadowed by Hollywood. And British theatre continues to live up to its reputation as the finest in the world; London's West End is the international centre for performing arts – whatever New Yorkers say!

Cinema, Theatre & TV

As seen on screen

The British cinema industry has its **ups and downs** (high points and low points), but the directors never fail to produce a wide range of films that are witty, challenging or just downright good. A common characteristic of British films is their reliance on dialogue or characterisation rather than computer-generated imagery and endless special effects – one happy outcome of low budgets and tough conditions.

Note that Brits talk more about **films** than movies, even though the latter term is sometimes favoured by aficionados. Likewise, the US term 'movie theatre' is rarely used; Brits go to the **cinema**.

Some other cinema-related terms include:

concession this means a discount. **Concession tickets** are cheaper tickets available at the cinema or theatre for senior citizens and students.

"FLICKS, PICTURES – FILMS"

flicks an old-fashioned term for the cinema ('Are you going to the flicks with us tonight?'), so called because the images used to flicker on the screen. Hence **Brit-flick** – a British-made film.

pictures another old-fashioned term for the cinema ('Are you going to the pictures with us tonight?')

trailer a preview (of an upcoming film) shown before the main film. Yep, the trailers come first.

> "GROUNDLINGS – THE STANDING AUDIENCE AT A SHAKESPEARE PLAY"

Treading the boards

The shows of the **West End** (central London's theatre district; Britain's version of America's Broadway) are the best known, but great drama, comedy and musicals can be seen at theatres in towns and cities across the country. Theatre-related terms in Britain include:

corpsing when an actor gets a fit of the giggles and can't continue with their lines

gods the upper balconies of a theatre, so called because they're so high up you're near heaven. Seats here are usually the cheapest, and the last to be sold because the view of the stage can be poor.

pantomime a light-hearted theatrical performance, in which a fairy tale or nursery story (Cinderella, Little Red Riding Hood, Babes in the Wood etc) is dramatised – usually with music and dancing, frequent ad-libbing and numerous contemporary references. Pantomimes are a favourite form of family entertainment during the Christmas and New Year season. And despite the name, they are not done in mime.

stalls seats on the floor of a theatre, as opposed to in the balcony

Sound & vision

TV and radio broadcasting in Britain used to be dominated by the **British Broadcasting Corporation** (BBC), a venerable and much-loved national public service institution. However, the Broadcasting Act of 1990 started the process of deregulation of radio and TV, meaning more and more TV channels and radio stations became available to the viewing and listening public. There are now four main terrestrial TV players with various channels – the BBC, ITV, Channel 4 and Channel 5 – while BSkyB absolutely dominates the pay satellite TV market (its closest rival being Richard Branson's Virgin). There are now hundreds of other niche channels on offer which show everything from cookery and classic comedy shows to shopping channels where you can buy everything from make-up to power tools. Between

ALL AROUND THE GLOBE

The famous **Globe Theatre** on London's South Bank is forever associated with Britain's best-known playwright, **William Shakespeare**. The original Globe Playhouse was built in 1598–99 and closed in 1642, just 26 years after Shakespeare's death.

In 1997 a replica Globe Theatre opened very close to the original location. It was constructed to reflect the original as closely as possible, and so performances take place under the open sky, with seating **in the round** (circling the stage) on wooden benches for an audience of 1000 and standing room for 500 **groundlings**.

2008 and 2012 Britain switched over from analogue to digital TV, while sales of HD (High Definition) and 3-D television sets continue to grow. These days, an Englishman's home is not so much his castle but a multimedia entertainment hub.

> “telly
> – television set”

Some other terms relating to English broadcasting include:

Auntie term of endearment for the BBC

Beeb another term of endearment for the BBC

chat show a TV show based around entertaining interviews, rather than, say, news or music

dumbed down an accusation frequently levelled at TV producers on free-to-air channels, meaning that they've dropped the quality of their programmes in order to chase ratings, in the face of competition from cable and satellite stations

programme what the Americans call a TV or radio 'show', the Brits generally call a programme

tabloid television TV programmes that ape the style and tone of popular (or 'tabloid') newspapers – short on analysis, hot on gossip

telly television set

watershed the time in the evening after which there are fewer restrictions on TV content. It's currently 9pm or 9.30pm – on the assumption that children are safely tucked up in bed and won't be exposed to post-watershed swearing, violence and nudity.

Music & clubs

Britain has long been a major player in pop and rock music. Although America led the way in the years after World War II, by the 1960s Britain was getting in on the act, with early exports including the Beatles, the Rolling Stones, the Who, the Kinks and Welsh soul-man Tom Jones.

By the 1970s, a notable genre of British music was **glam rock**, exemplified by stardust-speckled heroes like Marc Bolan and David Bowie. **Prog rock** (progressive rock) was another genre of the time, incorporating features of jazz and classical music. By the early '80s, however, prog rock heroes such as Genesis, Pink Floyd and Led Zeppelin were considered outdated, self-indulgent **dinosaur bands**. The new sound was **punk music** – energetic, anarchic and with a DIY approach ('Here's three chords, now form a band' ran a famous quote in a **fanzine**) – and it returned pop to the grassroots, at least for a while. Notable British punk bands included the Sex Pistols (famous for one album and a clutch of mostly banned singles), the Clash, the Damned and the Buzzcocks.

Then punk begat another genre: **new wave** (ie everything that was a bit punky), with leading exponents including the Jam, the Tourists and Elvis Costello.

Around this time, another British speciality – **heavy metal** – enjoyed an upsurge, with bands such as Black Sabbath (featuring Ozzy Osbourne) and Judas Priest exporting soulful melodies and intriguing interpretations of established religion to concert halls full of **headbangers** worldwide.

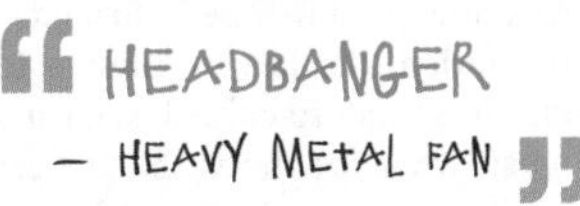

DON'T BOOB

The American term 'boob tube' is not used in Britain to mean 'television'. In Britain, **boobs** is slang for breasts, and a **boob tube** is a tight-fitting strapless top. **Boob** also means mistake, which is what you'd be making if you used this term in the wrong context.

The 1980s also saw a surge of **electronica** being produced by the likes of Depeche Mode, Cabaret Voltaire and Human League. It overlapped with the **New Romantic** scene, which featured bands such as Spandau Ballet, Duran Duran and Culture Club – all frills and fringes, and a definite swing of pop's pendulum away from the untidy punks.

In 1983 in the musical hotbed of Manchester, arguably Britain's second city, a band called New Order (formed from the ashes of Joy Division) released the seminal track 'Blue Monday', combining the guitar sound of punk with the pulsating beat of a new sound called **dance**. This fed into the development of the British **rave** scene, with music influenced by the US **house** genre.

The heady mix of dance and rock music peaked in the late '80s to early '90s, still centred on Manchester and epitomised by bands like the Stone Roses and the Happy Mondays. It became known simply as the **Manchester sound**, or **Madchester**.

The '90s also saw the renaissance of **indie** bands (from 'independent'). The likes of Blur, Supergrass, Ocean Colour Scene, Manic Street Preachers Pulp, and Oasis revived the flagging guitar-based format. Heralded as the **Britpop** revolution, it's largely thanks to these bands that the indie guitar sound remained such a major feature of British pop music when it entered the 21st century.

Other British musical genres of the late 1990s and early 2000s include **breakbeat** or **nu skool breakbeat** and **house** and **drum and bass**.

bhangra the name for a style of traditional music from the Punjab region of South Asia; in recent times it's also become the term for a style of music invented in Britain (though now exported around the world), which mixes traditional Punjabi styles with modern pop, rap, dance and reggae music – among others

drum and bass dance music emphasising fast, heavy beats and strong bass; also known as **jungle**. Originally a British genre, though it spread quickly. Influences on drum and bass include **oldskool** rave, house, techno, hip-hop and even ragga (a type of electronic reggae).

grime a very hardcore mix of **garage** and **drum and bass**. Usually has fast rough beats and often very explicit or provocative vocals.

trip-hop a musical style derived from hip-hop but slower in tempo, pioneered most notably by bands and artists from the city of Bristol, such as Massive Attack, Portishead and Tricky. Also known as the **Bristol sound**.

THE PROMS

The best known of all British classical music concert programmes is **the Proms** (short for 'promenade concerts' because people used to walk about, or stand, while they listened). It's one of the world's greatest music festivals. Concerts are held from mid-July to mid-September each year at the Royal Albert Hall in London, and are widely broadcast on TV and radio.

The US term 'prom' is not used in Britain – the Proms have nothing to do with high-school dances.

UK garage also known as 2 step. Whereas the US garage sound is nearer house music and has an emphasis on vocal melodies, the UK version includes more influences from hip-hop and urban street culture.

> "trip-hop
> – music style related to hip-hop"

Going out clubbing

The coverage above of dance music genres brings us inevitably to the world of clubs. In Britain, London is indisputably the number one spot for clubbing, but the cities of Brighton, Bristol, Cardiff, Nottingham, Glasgow, Manchester, Sheffield, Swansea, Edinburgh, Leeds and Liverpool all have large and thriving club scenes as well, where top DJs and wild theme nights bring in eager clubbers to enjoy tracks, tunes and cuts – a lot of them on vinyl ('old-fashioned' records as opposed to CDs or other digital media).

In British club terminology, club doesn't necessarily refer to a place. (The place is also called a venue.) A club can be an entity encapsulating the regular DJs and punters (customers), the type of music, the overriding theme and the general vibe. This is also called a club night, simply a night, or a session (eg 'a breaks night'). Just to keep you on your toes, some club names and venue names are synonymous. Others aren't.

A small selection of live music and club terms you may hear include:

B-boy originally a US term for a breakdancer; in the UK context it can refer to any hip-hop fan who looks the part

bouncer door steward at a club or venue (even some pubs), usually with the power to decide who can enter and who can't. The term can also mean a security steward within a club or concert employed to eject miscreants.

large in the context of clubbing or entertainment generally, **having a large one** (or simply **having it large**) is having a big night out. Hence also **larging it**.

mash-up a club mix putting together various styles of music

mosh pit the area in front of the stage at a live performance, where the fans dance most enthusiastically

phat cool; heavy

pills in the context of clubbing, pills usually means ecstasy. For example, the friendly stranger in the toilets may ask 'Need any pills?'

punters this word originally meant the people attending a horse-race (**to punt** means 'to bet'), but now refers to people at any event such as a rock concert or a club (eg 'On Gatecrasher's big nights there's always a long queue of punters trying to get in')

residency a DJ's regular (usually weekly or monthly) slot at a particular club

A BIT OF A SONG & DANCE

The Gaelic word **ceilidh** (pronounced 'kaylee'), meaning 'visit', originally referred to a social gathering in the home in Scotland. There'd be music and singing, and a local bard to relate poems, stories and legends. These days, a ceilidh means an organised evening of **folk** (traditional) entertainment, including music, singing and dance.

Festivals

Britain hosts a plethora of festivals, most - but not all - held in the summer when the weather is likely to be better. The list below (in alphabetical order) outlines a selection of the main events:

Bath International Music Festival top-class classical music and opera, plus jazz and world music (mid-May to early June, Bath)

Braemar Gathering with over 20,000 people, including the Royals, 'gathering' is an understatement for this famous Highland knees-up (first Saturday of September, Braemar, Deeside, in Scotland)

Chelsea Flower Show blooming marvellous floral feast (late May, London)

Edinburgh Fringe held concurrently with the Edinburgh International Festival, **the Fringe** offers hundreds of amateur and professional offbeat and avant-garde performances (August, Edinburgh)

Edinburgh International Festival one of the world's largest and most important arts festivals, overshadowed only by its own Fringe festival (August, Edinburgh)

Edinburgh Military Tattoo three weeks of pageantry and soldierly displays (August, Edinburgh)

Euro Pride Europe's largest gay and lesbian march and festival (late June to early July, London)

Glastonbury Festival huge open-air happening with hippy roots, involving three days of music, dance, camping – and, frequently, mud (late June, Somerset)

Glyndebourne Opera Festival world-class opera in a country-house garden (May to August, Lewes, Sussex)

Guy Fawkes Night firework and bonfire celebrations held to commemorate the failure, in the year 1605, of an

HIGHLAND GAMES

Held throughout the summer at towns and villages across Scotland, **highland games** involve music and dancing competitions and sporting events, such as **tossing the caber** (heaving a tree trunk as far as possible) and **throwing the hammer**. Originally, the games were organised by clan chiefs who'd recruit the strongest competitors for their army or bodyguard. Today, the winners just get the glory.

attempt to assassinate the king and Parliament (5 November, nationwide)

International Eisteddfod music festival bringing together a lively mix of cultures from Wales and far beyond (July, Llangollen)

Isle of Wight what started in 1968 with headliners Jefferson Airplane has turned into a major festival in recent years (June, Isle of Wight)

Jorvik Viking Festival horned helmets galore, plus mock invaders and Viking longship races (February, York)

Notting Hill Carnival a spectacular Caribbean-style multicultural feast (late August, London)

Reading Festival three-day open-air rock, pop and dance extravaganza (late August, Reading, Berkshire)

Royal Highland Show Scotland's national display-piece with big-horned cattle, cabers, bagpipes, kilts – the lot (late June, Edinburgh)

Royal Welsh Show national agricultural and cultural gathering (mid-July, Builth Wells)

Sesiwn Fawr three-day rock, folk and beer bash in the heart of Wales (July, Dollgellau)

Window shopping

In addition to music, cinema and theatre, shopping is a major entertainment or leisure activity in Britain, as in many countries. It's about so much more than simply buying necessities – although some people would say that a new tie, a new handbag or just one more pair of those nice-looking shoes in the window is an absolute necessity.

Here are some terms that are frequently used in the boutiques, supermarkets and high streets of Britain:

advert an abbreviation for **advertisement**, be it on TV, in a shop window or on a large **hoarding**. (The latter item is called a 'billboard' in the US.)

car-boot sale a public sale of old or unused household items, similar in principle to the 'garage sales' or sales that people hold in their driveways in other countries. However, the car-boot sale generally takes place in a car park or field on the edge of town, with everyone bringing the stuff they want to sell in the **boot** (that's 'trunk' to Americans) of their car. The original idea was to sell items out of the boot, but these days people spread them out on the ground or a table.

chemist a shop selling prescription and nonprescription medicines. Many other countries use the term 'pharmacy' (which is also used in Britain) or 'drug store'. As well as medicines, at most chemists you can usually buy perfume, cosmetics, soap and **toiletries** (stuff you might use in the bathroom). Larger **high street** chemists sell an even

OLD JOKES' HOME

Bill loans £6 to Ben. The next day Ben gives Bill an ill-looking octopus. Bill says, 'What's this?' Ben replies, 'It's that sick squid I owe you.' Say it out loud. Don't you just love wordplay?

broader range of goods, including ready-to-eat food and photographic supplies.

fiver a colloquial term for a five-pound note. (Brits also use the term **tenner**, but not 'twentier'.)

greengrocer a shop selling fruit and vegetables; also a person working in the shop

high street primary street or road in a town where the bulk of the shops are – the butcher, the baker, the greengrocer, the newsagent, the chemist and so on

Marks & Sparks nickname for one of the most popular department stores in Britain, Marks & Spencer

> "MARKS & SPARKS
> – A FAVOURITE DEPARTMENT STORE"

p (pronounced 'pee') the abbreviation for **pennies** or **pence**, and often used in everyday speech. So 50p is pronounced 'fifty pee'.

pound the main unit of currency in Britain, also called the **sterling pound** or **pound sterling**. There are 100 pennies in a pound.

queue a line of people, usually waiting to pay for something. In shops you'll see a sign saying 'Please queue here'. It's what Americans call a 'line'.

quid the slang term for pound/s – as in the unit of currency, not the weight. Always singular, as in 'Can you spare five quid?' or 'Twenty-five quid would do me fine'.

sale a period when everything in the shop, or most things, have cheaper than usual prices. Shops put up posters saying 'Sale'. The **January sales** is the period after Christmas when many shops reduce prices to clear stock. The term **on sale**, however, just means that something is available.

Clothes

Visitors to Britain may see items advertised for sale and wonder what they are. Here are some peculiarly British terms for items of clothing, and a few other items, with their definitions or translations:

anorak a hooded weatherproof jacket

cagoul a jacket, usually made of nylon and waterproof and breathable (thanks to a high-tech 'membrane' fabric attached to the nylon). Originally developed for hikers and outdoor enthusiasts, this type of garment is now worn by city types around town as well.

dressing gown what you might wear to cover your body or pyjamas between bedroom and bathroom, or just while getting properly dressed; called a 'bathrobe' in the US. In British English, the term refers to the silky or thick cotton variety.

jumper woollen sweater

knickers women's underpants

mackintosh raincoat; often shortened to **mac**

pants underpants (whether for men or women). In British English it does not mean 'trousers', as in the US or Australia. The word **pants** is also a slang term for 'bad' or 'useless'.

suspenders technically, suspenders are the strips of elastic attached to a **suspender belt** which hold up **stockings**, but the term is often used to mean 'suspender belt' ('I was standing there in my bra, pants and suspenders when some guy just strolled into the changing room').

PANTS JOKE

What's the difference between a man running and a dog running? The man wears trousers and the dog pants.

More wonderful British wordplay.

trainers short for 'training shoes', meaning gym/tennis/jogging shoes; often called 'sneakers' in US English and 'runners' in Australian English

trousers leg-wear for both men and women. These are what Americans call 'pants'.

vest in Britain this is a short-sleeved or sleeveless undershirt. A mother may say to children: 'It's cold today, so you'd better put a vest on'.

waistcoat a close-fitting, sleeveless, buttoned garment often worn under a suit or formal jacket, over a shirt. Called a 'vest' in the US.

Wellington boots high rubber boots; often shortened to simply **Wellingtons** or **wellies**. They were named after the Duke of Wellington (1769–1852), the great general and statesman who defeated Napoleon in the Battle of Waterloo. Although his boots were leather. They're also sometimes called **gumboots** (a term more familiar in other English-speaking countries).

SLANG & MISUNDERSTANDINGS

Mad as a box of frogs

Look out for these...

CLASSIC PHRASE:

COR BLIMEY!

An old-school exclamation originally invented to replace the blasphemous 'God blind me'

TRY THIS ONE:

BONKERS

A typically English term for being eccentric or mad

USE WITH CAUTION:

SUSS

Depending on how it's used this word can signify something suspicious, someone well informed or something well organised

MISUNDERSTANDINGS:

I PISSED IN MY WELLIES

Not to be taken literally – it means 'I took precautions but they didn't work'

SLANG

British English is often mischievous and outrageous, and boasts a vast vocabulary of slang and colloquialisms. Some linguists estimate that British English contains around 20,000 slang terms (although many of these originate in America or other English-speaking countries), so it would be impossible to cover them all in this book.

Some slang words and colloquial expressions are widely used across Britain. Others are less well known, or only used in certain areas. In the same way, some colloquial words have been with us for centuries – the first recorded use of **booze**, for example, occurred in the 14th century, and the term **jet set** may derive from Chaucer's use of **jet** to mean 'fashion' in the Canterbury Tales. Other slang terms seem to be invented overnight, only to disappear from use just as suddenly. Keep in mind that slang changes constantly, and even some of the phrases in this book may have fallen out of use by the time you read it.

Everyday slang

Most linguists agree there's a distinction between slang and colloquial (ie informal) speech, but few agree on exactly where the distinction lies! Generally, slang is 'harder' – facetious, insulting, vindictive, or all three! – but there's a great deal of overlap between British slang and colloquial speech. Most of the terms listed in this section are acceptable in all but the most formal of situations; we've tried to indicate any that would be avoided in polite company.

aggro trouble; violence; hooliganism; an argument; a fight. (From 'aggression' or 'aggravation', and often spelt 'agro'.) The word is used as a noun in British English; for example, 'There was a lot of aggro when two rival gangs of football supporters met in the street'. It's not used as an adjective as in Australian English: Brits wouldn't say 'Don't be so aggro'.

argy-bargy (pronounced 'ahjy bahjy') an argument; a fight; wrangling. As in 'There was a bit of argy-bargy down the pub last night – two blokes arguing over a pool match'. The term was used to great effect by tabloid newspapers in the 1980s when Britain went to war against Argentina over possession of the Falkland Islands.

ASBO/asbo an acronym for Anti-Social Behaviour Order, an order introduced in 2005 to help police combat hooliganism and petty crime ('I was caught stealing from a shop, and had an ASBO slapped on me'). It has developed into a (lower-case) byword for a control device, as in 'This car is so powerful it doesn't just need good brakes, it needs an asbo' or 'The team played an aggressive match worthy of an asbo'. It also quickly became a verb: 'Steve's been asboed so he can't come out tonight'.

banger an old car in poor condition

bangers sausages

beeswax business ('What I do with my money is none of your beeswax'). Sometimes spelt and pronounced 'bizwax'.

bent corrupt or illegal. The word is also derogatory slang for homosexual.

bill the police, as in 'Watch out, here comes the bill'. Also often **the old bill**.

blessshort for 'bless them', or 'bless her'; normally used in the context of children or babies, meaning something like 'How sweet' or 'She's so cute'

blimey often combined with **cor** to form **Cor blimey!** – an expression of surprise. (Originally invented to replace the blasphemous phrase 'God blind me'.)

bloody-minded intentionally difficult; obstinate, persistent, stubborn

blotto so tired as to be unable to think. Also means drunk ('I feel absolutely blotto').

"KNACKERED
– EXHAUSTED"

bobby police officer. The term comes from Robert Peel, the British Prime Minister who established the Metropolitan Police Force in 1828. Newspapers frequently call for 'More bobbies on the beat'.

bodge an ineffective or poor-quality repair, as in 'The plumber came to fix my shower, but made a real bodge of the job, and it still leaks'. It's also used as a verb: 'I tried to bodge my broken exhaust pipe with a bit of wire, but it still fell off'.

bonk to have sex ('Don't go in there, Arthur and Sharon are **bonking**')

bonkers mad

boob colloquial term for mistake (eg 'I asked if it was his daughter, but it was his girlfriend. I made a major boob there.')

boobs colloquial term for breasts

botch to fail or make a mistake ('I really botched my driving test'). Also used synonymously with **bodge**.

bottle bravery, courage ('He doesn't have the bottle to ask her'). Hence, **lost your bottle** means you're scared.

brilliant cool, great ('You should see my new trainers, they're brilliant').

bum backside; buttocks ('After driving all day, my bum was aching'). A much more acceptable term than **arse**; advertisements for a brand of soft toilet paper even feature the strapline 'Be kind to your bum'. **Bum** also means 'to borrow' or 'scrounge'; for example, 'Can I bum a couple of quid off you?' or 'Can I bum a fag off you?' – the latter translating as 'Can you give me a cigarette?' in British English.

BYE-BYE BONK

The word **bonk** (referring to sexual intercourse) seems to have first emerged in the 1970s, and appeared in newspaper headlines of the 1980s as a conveniently short and sanitary substitute for another relevant four-letter word. In the same way, the term **plonker** first appeared in a TV show, invented to take the place of a less acceptable (but similar-sounding) word for 'fool' or 'idiot'. Both bonk and plonker have now passed into everyday use.

At one time, however, **bonk** had a different meaning. Some endurance athletes, particularly racing cyclists, would talk about 'getting the bonk', meaning they were very tired due to extended exertion (in the same way as a marathon runner might say they were 'hitting the wall'). Hence, the wise cyclist would carry some food in a **bonk bag**. Now that bonk has another connotation (still connected to exertion though), the earlier meaning has largely dropped out of use.

bung this means 'put', as in 'Just bung it in the oven'. It also means 'give', as in 'Do this for me and I'll bung a few quid your way'. As a noun, **bung** means 'a bribe', especially in a sporting context. A jockey might **take a bung** to hold a horse back and throw the results of a race, for example. In the 1990s, several major football matches were rigged after players received large **bungs**.

chat talk; gossip ('Let's sit down and have a chat')

chuffed delighted, pleased. Often used in the phrase **chuffed to bits**.

clever physically well, generally used in the negative: 'I don't feel too clever' means 'I'm sick'

cock-up error, mistake. This colourful compound word can also act as a verb ('Look what you did, you cocked up everything' or more often '...you cocked everything up').

crafty artful, clever, skilful; all with a slight implication of underhand behaviour

daft silly; mildly crazy

dead extremely, very. For example, 'I went to that new club last night. It was dead good.'

dodgy (the *o* is pronounced as in 'hot') awkward; questionable; unreliable ('I wouldn't buy that cheap watch: it looks dodgy'). Can also be used to describe a person: 'That Jimmy's always got the police calling round; he's a bit of a dodgy character'.

dole financial aid provided to the unemployed by the state (often called 'welfare' in other countries). Being unemployed is hence often called being **on the dole**.

done cheated, tricked ('I was done out of 20 quid')

dosh (the *o* pronounced as in 'hot') money, cash

dotty feeble-minded, silly

drip a boring, uninspiring, weak or feeble person

fag cigarette ('I'm just popping out for a packet of fags')

fagged exhausted ('After working a 12-hour shift I was completely fagged'). Also **fagged out**.

fair enough okay, I agree, that's acceptable ('You said I was off work on Monday. Fair enough. But I worked overtime on Tuesday' or 'You want 250 quid for that old car? Fair enough, I'll take it.')

fiddle literally means 'to handle or play with using the fingers', often with negative connotations – 'I was fiddling with the computer and now it won't work' or 'Don't fiddle with your hair'. Hence, **fiddling about** has come to mean wasting time. **Fiddle** also means to cheat (to **fiddle the books**, for example, is to falsify the accounts).

flog sell

gob mouth, hence **gobsmacked** (meaning surprised; eg 'Little Sammy had refused to eat vegetables for years, so I was completely gobsmacked when he suddenly started wolfing them down'). Also **gobshite**, a vulgar term for someone who's cheeky, talks rubbish or simply talks too much.

"GOBSMACKED
– SURPRISED"

grand one thousand pounds (money), as in 'That new car cost me 20 grand'

grass to inform (usually the police) about someone's misdeeds. Hence **grassed up** means to be informed on, as in 'I was grassed up and now I'm in prison'.

jammy lucky

kip a nap or short sleep

knackered exhausted

lad a boy. In the plural it can also mean adult (or teenage) friends: 'He's okay, he's one of the lads' or 'I'm going down the pub for a pint with the lads'. In the singular, **lad** often has connotations of mischievousness, and means something like 'wise guy' – as in 'I didn't do well in school because I was too busy being a lad'. A **lad's mag** is a magazine featuring, among other things, cars, music, computer games and pictures of scantily clad women.

laugh (often pronounced 'laff') used as a noun, this can mean 'a good time', as in 'That party was a right laugh' or 'Let's go out and have a laugh'. **Having a laugh** can also mean 'joking', as in 'Are you having a laugh?' (meaning 'Are you serious?').

lolly money

lost the plot angry; confused; rambling; or all three ('Then Jimmy lost the plot completely and started shouting at everyone in the pub')

minder bodyguard

moolah money

naff tacky, unfashionable or uncool; **naff off**, however, means 'go away'. See the box on p130 for more.

ned hooligan, rowdy person, troublemaker. Possibly an acronym for 'noneducated delinquent'.

nick to steal ('The kids decided to nick sweets from the shop'). It also means 'to arrest' (Policeman: 'If you touch another drop, I'll nick you for drunk driving'), and **the nick** means the prison or the police station ('Take him down to the nick'). Thus, you might get a paragraph such as: 'A lad I know was nicking cars. Ended up getting nicked for it. Got taken down the nick, then did two years in Wormwood nick.'

nutcase silly or crazy person; often shortened to **nutter**

over the moon pleased, thrilled, very happy. Most famously used by football team managers on TV (Interviewer: 'How does it feel to win the match, Ron?' Manager: 'Me and the boys are over the moon, Trevor').

pad house or flat, as in 'This is a nice pad' or 'He lives alone in a trendy little bachelor pad'

ponce a derogatory term for an ostentatious or effeminate man (the word **nonce** has a similar meaning). Also, a lazy man living off his wife or girlfriend's earnings, and a verb meaning to borrow (usually inappropriately and permanently), as in 'He's always poncing money off me'.

NAFF IS NAFF

The word **naff** was widely used in Polari – the 'underground' slang language favoured by gay British men in the 1950s and 1960s (although its origins are much older). The word is commonly defined as an acronym of 'not available for fucking' which came to mean generally unavailable and then simply 'bad' before crossing into mainstream slang and acquiring its current meaning – tacky, unfashionable or uncool. In reality, naff may be derived from the noun **naffy**, meaning idiot or fool in some old dialects spoken in northern England, or from the Romany (Gypsy) word *naflo*, meaning broken or useless. People still remember Princess Anne shouting 'Naff off!' at a group of newspaper photographers, even though it happened in the 1980s. It's not clear if she knew the possible derivation of her outburst.

potty foolish, silly (but not as bad as 'crazy'), or very keen on something (eg 'She's potty about motorbikes')

as sick as a parrot originally a phrase coined by football players to express disappointment on suffering a defeat; now a general term meaning 'sad' or 'dispirited' (but not 'ill')

skint having no money (ie 'broke')

slippy slippery (as in an icy surface); or quick and evasive ('We can't catch that thief, he's a slippy character')

Sloane Ranger wealthy, well-connected young person, with the implication that they're also superficial and vacuous. Taken from Sloane Square, an expensive London shopping and residential district.

snog to kiss passionately; **a snog** is a long passionate kiss. Especially used by/about teenagers; also used humorously ('Come here and give me a good old snog').

sorted 'it's all sorted' means 'it's all arranged' or 'it's all fixed'

spondulicks money, pronounced 'spondoolicks' (**sponds** for short)

spot a portion, some. For example, 'a spot of tea', 'a spot of rain' or 'a spot of trouble'.

stumm quiet (pronounced 'stum' or 'shtoom'). **To keep stumm** means 'to keep quiet'. (From German *stumm*, meaning 'mute', via Yiddish.)

take the piss to mock; see also p142

telly television

tight mean with money (eg 'Oh come on, lend us a quid, don't be so tight')

whinge (rhymes with 'hinge') to whine or complain. For example, 'All the baby did was whinge all night' or 'That meeting was a real whinge-session'.

willy penis. Unlike other terms for the male organ, this word is fairly harmless and can be used in all but the politest company.

wind up (pronounced to rhyme with 'mind') as a verb it means 'to annoy', as in 'That music really winds me up'. As a noun, **wind-up**, it means either 'an annoyance' or 'a trick' ('He said it was the Prime Minister on the phone, but I knew it was a wind-up'). It does not mean 'to start' except in the context of clocks and watches.

wonga money

yummy mummy rich young mother with expensive baby accessories

yob like **ned**, a hooligan; troublemaker; or rowdy person. Also **yobbo**.

Street talk

One of the most interesting aspects of the list of 'street talk' that follows is just how many words mean 'good' or 'cool'. A similar number translate as 'bad' or 'uncool'. It's so typical of the English language; one word would do, but why stop there?

Increasingly, the new slang terms young British people adopt come from Australian and American English – not surprising, given the international nature of TV, music and cinema. Thus, although we've tried to concentrate on British terms, some of those listed below will be familiar to Americans and Australians already.

bafta good, cool

banging enjoyable, fun ('We had a banging time last night'); in the context of music, loud and hard (eg 'banging techno')

Beemer a BMW car

bender drinking spree

black good, cool

bling ostentatious jewellery, especially on men. (Originally a term applied to the adornments favoured by rap artists, now more widely applied.)

blood friend, mate (used predominantly by black youths in London). So 'Wassup, blood?' (meaning 'What's up, mate?') might be answered with 'Just hanging out with me bloods'.

boost to steal a car ('Kev boosted a Beemer last night')

bruv brother; meaning 'mate' (eg 'Wassup bruv?')

chav a term referring to one of an entire subculture of white working-class teenagers, characterised by: poverty; ill health; low education; violence; vandalism; the wearing of fake sportswear and cheap jewellery; the driving

SUSPECT DEVICES

The slang word **suss** can be used in various contexts. If something is uncertain or someone unclear in their intentions they might be described as suss (from 'suspect' or 'suspicious'). The **suss law** was a controversial law permitting police officers to stop and search suspicious people (the controversy centred on who was considered suspicious). From that came **suss out**, meaning first 'to investigate' (as in 'Let's suss out that guy'), and then simply 'to check' or 'to follow up' ('We need to suss out the route in advance' or 'That's a good suggestion, I'll suss it out'). Someone who knows something or is generally well informed was therefore said to be **sussed**, and from there sussed developed to mean 'properly organised' or simply 'good'. Thus, from being a pejorative word, suss has become a term of approval. It's now **well sussed**!

of poorly customised secondhand cars; the prodigious consumption of alcohol, cigarettes and junk food; and early reproduction. It's vaguely similar to the US concept of 'trailer trash'. The term is thought to derive from an old Romany (Gypsy) word for 'child', which later became an insult for adults. Its widespread modern usage is partly due to the popularity of the website www.chavscum.co.uk, which claims to offer 'a user's guide to Britain's new ruling class'. Chav has spawned words such as **chavettes, chavdom, chav-towns**.

class good, cool; attractive

decent good, cool; attractive

div dork, fool, idiot ('I feel such a div in this hat')

dope just the best

doss a noun meaning 'very easy' ('That exam – what a doss!'). Also a verb that means 'relax' or 'do nothing': 'I don't feel like going out tonight, so I'm just going to doss around at home'.

draw marijuana

filthy cool; extreme; wild. As in 'That tune's got some filthy bass on it' or 'We had a filthy time last night'.

fit attractive, sexy

gaff house, place to live (eg 'This is a nice gaff, mate')

gear recreational drugs

geezer this can mean simply 'man' or 'bloke' (eg 'Who's that geezer?'), or it can be used in place of 'mate' (eg 'Nice one, geezer!'), or to mean something like 'hustler' or 'wheeler-dealer' (eg 'He's a bit of a geezer, always getting money from somewhere')

gross awful, disgusting; ugly

GOING TO THE DOGS

Dogs are popular not only as pets in Britain but also for use in metaphors. A **dog's breakfast** is a mess or a weird mixture. The **dog's bollocks** is the opposite – it means great, top-quality, successful or the best, and is often shortened to **the dogs**, as in 'I went to that great new bar last night; it's the dogs'. (The **badger's nadgers** is preferred by some Brits. Both terms are coarse variants of the **bee's knees**.)

The amount of dog terminology in British slang can confuse foreigners. In the film *The 51st State*, for example, the American character played by Samuel L Jackson famously asks his British partner in crime 'Any dogs involved?'

"BENDER
– A DRINKING SPREE"

horizontal cool, relaxed, easy-going

innit? (ie 'isn't it?') a phrase which seems to seek corroboration but is actually just a way to round off any statement. For example, 'I hate the way she wears her hair, innit?' or 'We went to London last weekend, innit?'

jissum/jissom good, cool

kicking enjoyable, fun

lardarse overweight person

large a big night; cool; fun. Especially said of a party or club (eg 'Bob's party was well large.'). Hence **having it large** or **larging it**.

loved up high (usually on ecstasy)

lush good, tasty, attractive

messy generally used to mean 'eventful' and involving lots of drugs/alcohol/trouble (eg 'Last night was messy, man: I downed a pint of vodka and woke up in the park'). Can also refer to the effects of drugs: 'I just smoked a massive joint and I'm feeling a bit messy now'.

minger (rhymes with 'singer') an ugly person

minging (pronounced to rhyme with 'singing') unpleasant; ugly

mint good, cool, nice; attractive

moose unpleasant, boring; ugly person

nugget a £1 coin

pants bad; used both as an adjective ('This place has no atmosphere – it's pants') and an expletive ('Oh pants!')

pillock idiot, fool

puff marijuana

raasclart originally a Jamaican insult (possibly literally meaning 'arsecloth'); also used to describe black slang generally, especially as spoken by white wannabes. So someone might say, 'Look at those fucking chavs, giving it all that raasclart bollocks'.

rank disgusting, ugly

sad bad; unfashionable; unlikable. Often used as an insult; for example 'Sit down and shut up, you sad bastard'. The corresponding noun is **sadcase** or **saddo**.

safe excellent, cool

shandy someone who can't handle drink (it's also a type of drink that contains equal parts beer and lemonade)

sharp attractive; sexy; fashionable. Often used in a derogatory context: 'Never trust the guys in sharp suits'.

skank an unfashionable, badly dressed person. **To skank** is to steal or cheat.

> "MINGING
> – UGLY OR UNPLEASANT"

skanky ugly, smelly, dirty, foul

skeg an unfashionable, badly dressed person

sketchy drugged out; flaky, unreliable

skunk strong cannabis

smart good, cool; fashionable

A BIRD IN THE HAND...

British English slang words of yesteryear – still heard today in traditional songs – include **bird** and **bush**, meaning male and female genitals respectively, and shedding a whole new light on the phrase 'a bird in the hand is worth two in the bush'.

sorted good, cool; fashionable. Also, in the context of drugs, 'organised'. The guy outside the club might say, for example, 'You sorted for Es?' (ie ecstasy).

sound good, cool; fashionable

stomping enjoyable, fun

sucky dull, bad

tax steal

tightarse a person who's mean with money (not someone neurotic or anally retentive)

top excellent, cool; but also a verb **to top oneself** meaning 'to commit suicide' ('Life is so hard, sometimes I feel like topping myself')

twat an idiot (also an obscene term for female genitals). **To twat**, however, means to strike, hit or punch ('Shut the fuck up or I'll twat you').

twoc (pronounced 'twok') to steal a car and go joyriding (probably an acronym for 'take without consent')

well very. As in 'Let's go to Club X – the music's well good' or 'Don't annoy Billy, he's well hard'.

whizz speed (amphetamines)

wicked excellent, cool, exciting

yard house (eg 'I got the gear back at me yard, man'). From Jamaican English.

There are dozens of slang terms not included here. Street slang in particular goes in and out of fashion so quickly that if you try some of the above expressions on a young British person they may laugh and say something like 'That's sooooo last year' or 'Yeah, like whatever, grandad'.

Swear words & obscenities

Let's not **beat about the bush** – a lot of British English slang is obscene. It's usually best not to try out the words in this section in public! Having said that, what's considered unacceptable is constantly changing, and some expressions that were seriously obscene or blasphemous at one time have now become, if not acceptable, at least far less shocking.

The list below provides explanations or equivalents for just a small selection of British obscenities.

arse backside. Brits also use **ass** (as Americans do), which tends to be regarded as less offensive than arse. **To kick ass** means to 'get things moving' (or in some contexts, to be successful, eg 'Man United played a kick-ass game and won five-nil'); **a kick up the arse** means something like 'a reprimand' or a 'wake-up call'. The word arse also gives us **arsehole** (idiot; unpleasant person) and **arse-licker** (lackey, yes-man). The phrase **can't be arsed** means 'can't be bothered' (eg 'I intended going to go into town tonight, but now I can't be arsed').

bastard originally someone of illegitimate birth but now a general insult, as in 'Look at the damage you've done to my car, you stupid bastard'

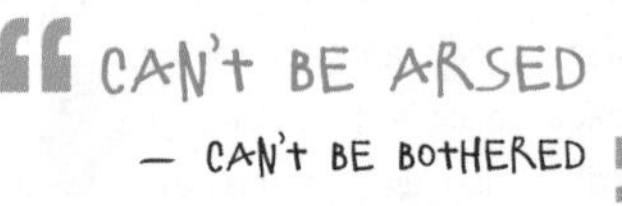

SLANG EVERY-BLOODY-WHERE

As well as cropping up very frequently between 'normal' words, British swearwords sometimes crop up between syllables, as in **abso-bloody-lutely**, meaning 'yes, I agree', or **halle-fucking-lujah**, in the context of celebration ('We finally got a pay rise – halle-fucking-lujah'). A favourite we once overheard was 'This pub is dirty and packed full of **hoi po-fucking-loi**' – neatly combining a phrase derived from ancient Greek with an Anglo-Saxon expletive.

bleeding same meaning as **bloody** (see below) but slightly less offensive ('You want to borrow my car? Not bleeding likely'). It was possibly originally a euphemism for **bloody** or another blasphemous term – perhaps 'Bleeding Heart'? – when these were considered genuine swearing.

bloody an all-purpose slang term, generally used for emphasis. So if the train was **bloody late**, it means it was very late, and if someone calls you a **bloody idiot** they mean something like a 'big idiot' or 'stupid idiot'. **He can bloody well wait** amounts to 'He can damn well wait', while **Not bloody likely** means 'very unlikely'. This swearword has its roots in medieval blasphemy: it was initially 'beloved lady' (ie 'I swear by/on the Virgin Mary').

Bloody hell! exclamation which is used to mean anything from 'Damn it!' to something milder like 'Wow!'

bollocks a vulgar term for testicles ('I was playing football and got kicked in the bollocks'), but also used as a general way to disagree with a statement: Tom: 'Are you scared?' Harry: 'Am I bollocks.' (It's the equivalent here of 'Am I hell'.) Likewise, 'That's a load of bollocks' means 'That's rubbish'.

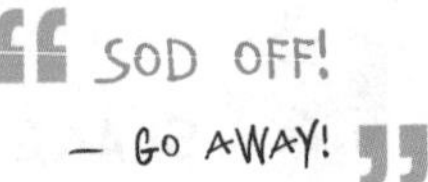

bugger originally this meant 'to have anal intercourse', but it's now a relatively inoffensive all-purpose insult (eg 'Don't leave it there, you stupid bugger'). It's also used to express surprise ('Well bugger me!') and in phrases such as 'Buggered if I know/care' (ie I don't know/care) or simply as a stand-alone expletive: eg 'Oh bugger!' instead of 'Oh fuck!', but not quite as bad. **To bugger** is also used to mean 'to break', 'foul up', 'ruin' or 'spoil' ('The engine's buggered'), and **I'm buggered** means 'I'm exhausted'. If someone tells you to **bugger off** they mean 'Go away!'

bugger all nothing ('He's got bugger all in the bank' or 'I give bugger all what you think')

crap slang for faeces (eg 'some bastard let their dog leave a big pile of crap on my lawn') but generally used to mean poor quality or simply bad ('I bought a new pair of boots down the market, but they were crap'), or to express disagreement (John: 'I can earn 500 quid a day cleaning cars'. Jim: 'That's crap' – ie, that's rubbish, that's untrue). It is generally not used as an expletive ('Oh crap, I'm late for work') as in American English.

cunt slang for the female genitals, and one of very few swearwords in British English to retain its full offensive power in most situations. It's used mainly as an insult, as in 'Some cunt's gone and nicked my car' or 'Come here and say that you little cunt'. Hence **cunted**, **cunting** and **cunt-ish**. In London and southern England particularly (where it's pronounced 'cahnt'), **cunt** is used almost as multifunctionally as **fuck**. However, it can also be used affectionately between blokes and **geezers** (eg 'Go and get the beers in, ya big cahnt').

fuck of Anglo-Saxon origins, **to fuck** is to have sex (also **to have a fuck**; and **a good fuck** is someone good in bed). It also means 'broken' or 'ruined' ('All my plans were **fucked** by this idiot') or 'drunk and/or in trouble' ('After 17 pints of lager, I was totally **fucked** last night'). Then there's **fuck up**, **fuck off**, **fucked off**, **fuck all**, **fuckwit**, phrases like **Fuck me** or **Fuck it**, and a lot more besides. **Fucking** is most commonly used either to mean 'very' ('I had a fucking brilliant holiday') or simply to replace 'er' and 'um'.

knackered tired, worn out

pissed drunk (not 'angry', as in American English)

pissed off angry

piss-up drunken session ('We had a great piss-up on Saturday night'); a variation is **on the piss** ('We had a great night on the piss on Saturday')

roger to have sex with, usually with implications of rough behaviour or unwillingness on the part of one partner. Also used (as with **fucked** and **buggered**) to mean 'broken' or 'damaged': 'Thanks to the way you drove my car, the gearbox is completely rogered'.

shag to have sex; slightly less vulgar than **fuck**. **Shagged** is also slang for 'tired' or 'worn out'.

WHAT THE?

It seems the British have been notoriously foul-mouthed for centuries – around 1400 Joan of Arc was calling the English **les goddams**. By the 1960s the French were calling the Brits **les fuckoffs** thanks to the large number of British people who base their conversation on the words fuck and fucking, with the occasional wanker or bastard thrown in for variety.

TAKING THE PISS

The slang word **piss** is another multifunctional marvel. Though its primary meaning is 'urine' or 'to urinate', **pissed** means 'drunk' and **pissed off** means 'angry'. Here are some other quaint phrases where it appears:

Are you taking the piss?
Are you mocking me?

He hasn't got a pot to piss in
He hasn't got anything/any money

I'm just pissing against the wind
This is a hopeless or difficult task

I pissed in my wellies
I took precautions but they didn't work

That pissed on your strawberries
That spoilt things for you

You couldn't organise a piss-up in a brewery
You can't do even the easiest task

shit faeces. **To shit** is thus 'to excrete'. Also a widely used slang term in British English meaning 'bad' ('That film was shit') or 'a bad person' ('Come here and say that, you little shit'). Also an expletive (eg 'Oh shit, here come the cops', whereas North Americans might say 'Oh crap...').

shithouse toilet (often used in the phrase 'He's as tough as a brick shithouse')

the shits diarrhoea (as in 'I got a bad case of the shits while travelling in India'); 'having the shits' doesn't mean 'angry' or 'annoyed' as in Australian English

sod a derogatory term derived from 'sodomy', but which now means something like 'idiot', 'fool', 'jerk' etc ('I saw you switch the cards, you crafty little sod'). It's even some-

times used with a touch of affection: 'George had to work all night to get the job done, poor old sod'.

Sod off! Go away!

Sod it! Damn it!

spunk sperm. This word and its derivatives – **spunky, a spunk, got some spunk** – is very rarely used in the contexts of bravery or sexual attraction, as it is in some other forms of English.

tosser fool, idiot. Used in a similar way, and has the same literal meaning, as **wanker** (see below), although it's less harsh ('Get yourself off home, you silly old tosser'). A variation is **tosspot** ('You've had too much to drink, you tosspot'). The phase **I don't give a toss** means 'I don't care'.

wanker fool, idiot. Depending on the context it can be a severe or mild insult: you might say 'You're a bunch of fucking wankers' to a group of rival football fans, but then you might say 'Come on, mate, don't be such a wanker, she's not worth crying over' to a friend. Derived from the word **wank**, literally meaning 'masturbate'.

REGIONAL VARIATIONS

Look out for these...

CLASSIC PHRASE:

WHERE THERE'S MUCK THERE'S BRASS

In Yorkshire they believe wherever there's dirt, there's money to be made

TRY THIS ONE:

USE YOUR LOAF!

'Loaf of bread' is cockney rhyming slang for 'head'; so 'use your loaf!' means 'use your head!'

USE WITH CAUTION:

SHAG

Local dialect for sandwich in Cumbria, but commonly used as a slang term for sex

MISUNDERSTANDINGS:

FOGGIE-BUMMERS AND HORNY-GOLLOCHS

Despite the vaguely sexual connotations, these are actually words for bumblebees and earwigs in the Aberdeen dialect

REGIONAL VARIATIONS

Say what?

English is spoken in many different ways throughout Britain, and some regional dialects can be mind-boggling for outsiders. Take, for example, the word for a small meal or snack. Depending on where you are in Britain this might be called your:

baggings	**dew-bit**	**nummet**
bait	**docky**	**nunch**
beaver	**dowen**	**nuncheon**
bite	**drum-up**	**progger**
biting	**jower**	**snap**
biting-on	**lowance**	**snapping**
bitings	**minning-on**	**tenner**

Here's another example; across Britain there are many regional terms for 'left-handed':

banh-handed	**gammy-pawed**	**kippie-fisted**
clicky-handed	**gawky-handed**	**pally-fisted**
corrie-fisted	**kack-handed**	**scrammy-handed**
corrie-flug	**kaggy-handed**	**scutchy-fisted**
cuddy-wifted	**kecky-handed**	**skerry-fisted**
cue-handed	**keggy-handed**	**skiffy-handed**

> "CLICKY-HANDED, CUDDY-WIFTED, SKERRY-FISTED
> – REGIONAL TERMS FOR LEFT-HANDED"

The other key feature of British English is the number of regional accents: even when the words are the same, they're pronounced very differently in different parts of the country. An inhabitant of Glasgow, for example, might have genuine difficulty understanding someone from rural Devon (and vice versa) when they're both using standard English expressions, before even getting on to any local dialect terms.

Visitors to Britain who speak English as a first language are often surprised when they experience difficulties communicating with people speaking in a regional dialect. Then, just as they're getting **the hang of** (used to) the dialect, they travel 50 miles (about 80km) down the road and are faced with a whole new set of words and pronunciations.

What's even more remarkable is that all these variations exist in a comparatively small area: Britain measures less than 1000 miles (under 1600km) from north to south, with an area only slightly larger than the US state of Pennsylvania or New Zealand's North Island.

Talk the talk

Most linguists agree that a regional dialect has three facets:

1. Specific words (that aren't used elsewhere). For example, **jag** is used in parts of Scotland to mean a medical injection, but out of context this would not be understood in other parts of Britain.

2. Sentence structure. In northern England, for example, the positions of pronouns or prepositions are sometimes

different from those in standard English. **I'll bring it you up** means 'I'll bring it up to you'.

3. Accent. That is, the way words are pronounced (whether they're local or standard English terms). For example, in southwest England the sound *s* is often pronounced more like a *z* (as in **Would you like beer or zider**?), while in London and the Southeast the letter *t* is frequently dropped from the middle of words and replaced with a glottal stop.

The terms 'dialect' and 'accent' are often used interchangeably, but this is misleading. Standard English can be spoken with a regional accent. When different words and sentence structures are used as well as the accent, then it's a dialect.

Accents & dialects

There are many areas within each region of Britain that have their own accents and dialect terms, subtly different from those of their neighbours. In Wales, for example, the accent of the English spoken in the city of Cardiff is different from the accent of Swansea around 30 miles (around 50km) along the coast. And both the city accents are different from the accent found in the farming lands of mid-Wales, and different again from the accent of the former mining valleys of South Wales. The experts can even tell the individual valley dialects apart; someone from Glynneath apparently has a slightly different lilt or turn of phrase from someone from the Rhondda area just 10 miles away.

Speaking in tongues

If you happen to be travelling around Britain, or if you meet a Brit travelling in your country, and you genuinely can't understand their local dialect, say so. Someone from an area where a donkey is called a **pronkus**, for instance, will almost always know the word 'donkey' as well. With the exception of a few elderly people who might find translation of this kind more difficult, most people are 'bi-dialectal' and can switch from their local dialect into standard British English, and will soften their accent as well for the sake of the weird foreigner who keeps saying 'Pardon?'

London & the southeast

The accents and dialects of English in London and southeast England are closest to what most non-British people will think of as typical English accents. They come in three principal flavours:

- the speech of the establishment and the middle and upper classes, known as **Received Pronunciation** (**RP**), and also called **BBC English**, **the Queen's English**, **Oxford English** or simply **posh English**
- an intermediate accent, falling somewhere between RP and cockney, called **Estuary English**, as it's spoken in the region around the estuary of the River Thames
- the working-class variety known as **cockney**

Posh English

Received Pronunciation (RP) needs little explanation. Think of English actors Hugh Grant in the film *Love Actually*, Patrick Stewart in *Star Trek: the Next Generation* or Emma Thompson in practically anything, and you've got the general idea.

Received Pronunciation was originally just one regional accent among many, and in fact originated to the north of London in the English Midlands. It became the accent of power and privilege as London grew in importance over the years. From the 18th century onward, wealthy families became ashamed of their regional accents and wanted to distinguish themselves from the local **yokels** (peasants, country bumpkins), and RP spread across the country. Today, it's widespread throughout Britain – sitting alongside regional accents in most areas – and is spoken especially by the upper classes.

You'll frequently hear that RP is the 'best', 'clearest' and 'most beautiful' accent of English, but these views are based on prejudice against other accents as much as anything. Increasingly, people in the south of England are moving away from RP speech because of its associations with old-fashioned class-based snobbery, and are turning instead to the accent midway between RP and cockney, which has become known as Estuary English.

Estuary English

Estuary English developed quite recently in the late 1970s or early 1980s. It's perceived as an 'everyman' accent – not posh like RP, but not as 'common' as pure cockney, although it uses features of both.

The popularity (and importance) of Estuary English is such that British leader Tony Blair – among several other politicians – used Estuary pronunciations in his speeches of the 1990s. This included introducing glottal stops into phrases such as 'a better Britain' so it came out more like 'be-er Bri-un' – the *t* is replaced with a sound like the one between 'uh' and 'oh' in 'uh-oh'.

GIVE US A BREAK

Many English dialects use a plural pronoun where the singular would normally be used, especially dialects in the north and Midlands. For example: **our kid** (my child), **our mam** (my mother), **our lass** (my wife), **give it us** (give it to me), **Do you really love us?** (Do you really love me?).

The word us is also often used where 'our' would appear in standard English. **Give her us best wishes** means 'Give her our best wishes'.

> "TITFER
> – HAT"

This technique is particularly interesting, as until the 1960s (or even later) politicians from beyond London would often drop their regional accents in favour of RP in order to be accepted by their colleagues. In contrast, Mr Blair's natural accent is close to RP and it seems he roughened it a little so as to appear more of a 'man of the people'.

Cockney

Traditionally, a true cockney is someone born within the sound of Bow Bells – the bells of the church of St Mary-le-Bow in the heart of London – but these days the term is more loosely applied to people from anywhere in London, and cockney is the name of the predominant accent of the entire city and surrounding area.

Key features of cockney pronunciation include the heavy use of glottal stops instead of the letter *t* in words like 'butter', 'Battersea' or 'lottery' and the dropping of *h* at the beginning of words like 'hurry', 'Harry' or 'Hampstead Heath' (in cockney, 'Amsted Eeth'). The letter *l* can often sound like *w*, as in 'miwk' for 'milk'. The *r* sound also becomes more like a *w* so that 'free', for example, can often sound like 'fwee'. The *th* sound in words like 'thought' and 'mother' are replaced with *f* and *v*, making these words sound like 'fort' and 'muvva'.

Cockney is probably best known for its **rhyming slang** – in which everyday words are replaced by words or phrases that rhyme with the original. Thus 'feet' become **plates of meat**. In many cases, however, just the first part of the slang phrase is used, so the slang for 'feet' is **plates** (eg 'These new shoes are killing me plates'). Sometimes the spelling of the slang term changes slightly too. For example, the slang for 'hat' is **tit for tat**, but this gets shortened to **titfer**.

There are numerous theories on the origin of rhyming slang. It could be something to do with thieves needing a secret language that the police couldn't understand. It could be just a way of confusing all outsiders. If the latter, it still works. Some of the more modern terms, though, seem a touch **skinned** (**skinned alive** – contrived).

Below is a selection of cockney rhyming slang. It may seem long and confusing, but don't worry – the average Londoner doesn't use very much rhyming slang in day-to-day conversation, and when it is used the meaning is usually clear from the context.

Adam and Eve	believe
apples and pears	stairs
April Fool	stool
Aristotle	bottle
army and navy	gravy
Artful Dodger	lodger
Auntie Ella	umbrella
babbling brook	crook (ie thief)
bacon and eggs	legs (often shortened to **bacons**)
ball of chalk	walk

MODERN COCKNEY

Relatively recent additions to the rhyming slang lexicon include **Daily Mail** for 'tale' (as in 'I don't believe a word of his daily') and **Harvey Nichols** for 'pickles' ('You got any Harveys to go with this cheese?'). Another recent addition is **Britney Spears** for 'beers', giving us sentences like 'Go and get the Britneys in'.

Barnaby Rudge	judge
Barnet Fair	hair (always shortened to **barnet**)
bat and wicket	ticket
Bath bun	sun
bees and honey	money
beggar my neighbour	labour
Bo Peep	sleep
boat race	face
bread and butter	gutter
bread and cheese	sneeze
bucket and pail	jail
burnt cinder	window
butcher's hook	look (shortened to **butcher's**)

> 'LET'S HAVE A BUTCHER'S, ME OLD CHINA'
>
> – 'LET'S HAVE A LOOK, MATE'

Cain and Abel	table
Cape of Good Hope	soap
Captain Cook	book
cash and carried	married
cat and mouse	house
china plate	mate ('How's it going, me old china?')
cobblers' awls	balls ('It's a load of cobblers')

cock linnet	minute
country cousin	dozen
currant bun	son
daisy roots	boots
dickory dock	clock
dicky bird	word
dig in the grave	shave
dog and bone	phone ('Get on the dog and call us a taxi')
dustbin lid	kid
elephant's trunk	drunk
field of wheat	street
fisherman's daughter	water
frog and toad	road
gay and frisky	whisky
ginger beer	queer
Glasgow Ranger	stranger
goose's neck	cheque
Harry Randall	candle
holy friar	liar
Isle of Wight	right
Jack Jones	alone ('I'm all on me Jack tonight')
Jimmy Riddle	piddle
Joanna	piano ('Let's have a tune on the old Joanna')
Khyber Pass	arse
Lillian Gish	fish
loaf of bread	head ('Don't be daft, use your loaf')

> 'COULD YOU ADAM AND EVE IT?'
> – 'COULD YOU BELIEVE IT?'

merchant banker	wanker
Mutt and Jeff	deaf (often shortened to **Mutt an'**, which sounds like 'mutton')
north and south	mouth
pen and ink	stink ('That cheese pens a bit')
pimple and blotch	scotch
plates of meat	feet
pleasure and pain	rain
pony and trap	crap
pork pies	lies (shortened to **porkies**)
rabbit and pork	talk ('He was rabbiting on for hours')
raspberry ripples	nipples
Richard the Third	turd
rub-a-dub-dub	pub
Scapa Flow	go ('Quick, let's scarper')
Sexton Blake	cake
skin and blister	sister
stand at ease	cheese
tiddly wink	drink
tin flute	suit
tit for tat	hat

Southwest England

The southwestern part of England is generally held to mean the long arm of land extending from the counties of Hampshire, Wiltshire and Gloucestershire through Somerset and Dorset to Devon and finally Cornwall. This region is called by some the **Westcountry** (one word) or the **Southwest Peninsula** - especially once you get west of Bristol.

The far western reaches of this region are almost as distant from London as the northern counties of Cumbria and Northumberland, and as a result the local speech has remained distinct and features of much earlier forms of English are still evident.

In addition, the English spoken in Cornwall features some words from Cornish, a Celtic language related to Welsh and Breton. Examples are **clicky-handed** ('left-handed', from Cornish *glikin*, 'left') and **whidden** ('runt' or 'weakling', in a litter of pigs for example - from Cornish *gwyn*, meaning 'white'). The word **fossick** ('to search or root around', as in 'She was fossicking around in my sock drawer') is also Cornish in origin but now used in other parts of Britain.

COVER YOUR MINCE PIES

Political correctness hasn't had much effect on rhyming slang – the term **trouble and strife** is still used for **wife**. And it doesn't shy away from vulgarity either – a woman's **Bristols** are her breasts (**Bristol City** is a football team, thus **Bristol Cities** equals **titties**). On the other hand, it's also used to euphemise: **love a duck** is rhyming slang for a popular expletive.

The southwest 'zee'

The features of the accent of southwest England include a pronounced *r* sound and a drawn-out *a* sound - so words like 'farmyard' are doubly affected. The *i* tends to sound more like *oi*, as well - the word 'tie' is pronounced more like 'toy'. The sound *s* often becomes *z*, such that the county of Somerset is jokingly spelt 'Zummerzet'. The *th* sound, too, is often pronounced *d*, so you might hear 'Dat's de end of my story' or possibly words like **dree** (three) and **droat** (throat). Another feature is the occasional switching of sounds, so that 'crisp' is **crips**, 'clasp' is **claps**, 'rich' is **urch** and 'red' is **urd**.

> "OO AAR, OI LOIKES ZOIDER!
> – I LIKE CIDER!"

The southwest accent is invariably adopted by other Brits when they're trying to imitate a farmer or country bumpkin: 'Oo aar, oi loikes zoider, oi does'. This stereotype actually goes back a long way. In Shakespeare's *King Lear*, for example, Edgar, the son of the Earl of Gloucester, has disguised himself as a peasant and adopts an appropriate accent:

'Ch'ill not let go, zir, without vurther 'casion... Good gentleman, go your gait, and let poor volk pass. An chud ha' bin zwaggered out of my life, 'twould not ha' bin zo long as 'tis by a vortnight.'

The first word **Ch'ill** (meaning 'I will') comes from 'Ich will'. Despite its German appearance, using **Ich** for 'I' was quite common in southwest parts into recent times. You'll also notice that the *s* has become *z* (zir, zwaggered, zo), and *f* has become *v* (vurther, volk, vortnight), both still features of southwestern English today.

Among the dialects of southwest England you'll also occasionally hear remnants of older forms of English grammar, such as **be** and **bist** meaning 'is' and 'are' (so **he be** means 'he is'; **ee bist** means 'you are') and **baint** meaning 'won't'. The word for 'him' is **er** and for 'them' is **mun**, as in **Er knawed mun well** – 'He knew them well'.

And finally, a habit unique to the southwest – especially in and around Bristol – is dropping the *l* from the end of words and adding an *l* where originally there wasn't one. So 'mangle' and 'mackerel' become 'mango' and 'macrow', and 'idea' becomes 'ideal' (What's the big ideal?).

Southwest words

The southwest is of course a very large region, and there are many variations within it. The rural accent of Wiltshire is different from the accent in Cornwall, for example; the urban accents of Bristol or Plymouth are different again. The examples of dialect words that follow are drawn mostly from Devon English, but can usually be found across the southwest.

argify	(pronounced 'argiffeye') argue
assards	backwards
auncy	(pronounced 'aunsee') anxious
bay-spittle	honey (lit: 'bee-spit')
bird	term of endearment to people of either sex
braksis	breakfast
caal	think (eg **What do ee caal you'm doing?** – 'What do you think you're doing?')
casn	cannot
dane	red-haired man
drumbledrane	bumblebee
emmet	ant

CELTIC PENGUIN?

There's a theory that the word 'penguin' (referring to the flightless seabird of the southern hemisphere) derives from the Cornish or Welsh *pen gwyn*, meaning 'white head'. It's thought that the term was originally applied to another flightless aquatic bird, the now-extinct Great Auk of the North Atlantic, which looked a bit like a penguin.

galley	to frighten, alarm (**Did er galley you?** – 'Did he frighten you?')
girt	great (ie large)
grockle	holidaymaker; visitor
grubbish	hungry
kaky	sticky
laceing	huge
mort	a lot (**There's a mort o' volk up church** – 'There's a lot of people up at the church')
pitching	settling of snow
pluff	unwell
shrammed	(to be) cold
shug	shy
sketchy	strange, odd
spun out	angry
suent	smooth
tempt	touch (**Doant ee tempt it!** – 'Don't you touch it!')
woppit	a blow (**Er geed un a woppit roun yurrole** – 'He gave him a hit round the earhole')
yucks	hiccups

West Midlands

As the name suggests, the Midlands is the central part of England. It's divided into two parts, the East Midlands and the West Midlands: the West Midlands is centred roughly on the city of Birmingham.

Birmingham (known fondly as **Brum** by the people who live there) is the second-largest city in Britain after London. Despite its size and its importance to the national economy, its inhabitants (known as **Brummies**) tend to get something of a bad press – and it's all thanks to their accent.

It's awroit

One of the key features of the West Midlands accent is vowels which are 'lowered' – so 'me' sounds like 'may', and 'you' is pronounced 'yow'. The words 'right' and 'price' are 'roit' and 'proice', while 'fate' and 'tame' can sound more like 'fight' and 'time'.

The vowel in words like 'it' and 'bit' is more drawn out into an *ee* sound, so they sound like the words 'eat' and 'beat'. The *s* sound becomes something between a standard *s* and a *z*: 'bus' is pronounced more like 'buzz'. Also, as in many urban accents of British English, most of the time *h* is either dropped from the start of words altogether or softened (so that 'home', for example, becomes more like 'whum').

THE SOUTHWEST

The Westcountry habit of adding an *l* to the end of some words has resulted in a name-change for the region's largest city. It was originally called **Bristow** – from 'Bridgestow', meaning a crossing on the river where boats tied up and unloaded – but the *l* was added and **Bristol** eventually became the official name and spelling.

Surely, there's nothing intrinsically unattractive about this accent. The negativity about it probably has more to do with the negative perceptions of the heavily industrialised West Midlands region. But then, Brummies themselves will pay their accent a backhanded compliment by saying that it's beautiful compared to the one in the area near Birmingham known as the **Black Country** (Dudley, Walsall, Wolverhampton). The Black Country folks, in response, say that Brum is just a watered-down version of the 'true' Midlands dialect.

Variations of the Brummie accent also can be heard in the rural – and very picturesque – counties of Staffordshire, Warwickshire and Hereford & Worcester, which surround the urban West Midlands.

> GOT A NARK ON
> — ANNOYED

West Midlands words

The expressions below may be heard generally around the Midlands, but especially in Birmingham and the Black Country.

adrenchen	soaking wet
am	is, are (hence **you am, we am** – usually shortened to **we'm** – and **am ya?**)
anent	against; next to
bab	baby, love, darling (as an endearment)
backen	to delay; to keep back
bad	ill
bin	am (**I bin** – I am)
bist	are you (eg **Weer bist?** – Where are you?); probably a shortening of **be thee** or **bin thee**

BAD PRESS

The words **Brum** and **Brummie** apparently derive from **Brummagem** (an old dialect name of **Birmingham**). The accent is not admired outside the region, and to make matters worse the *Oxford Dictionary* has an additional definition for the word **brum**: 'counterfeit, cheap and showy'.

bonk	small hill (see **tacky-bonk**)
Bostin!	Great! Super!
caggy-handed	left-handed
chunter	mutter or mumble; grumble
clemmed	hungry
cob	bread roll
cob it	throw it away
cod	to joke, to tease (**You'm coddin' me!** – You're joking!)
coost	could you (the negative is **coosn't**)
cost	can you (the negative is **cosn't**)
croggin' in	jumping the queue
donnies	hands (perhaps from French **donner**, 'to give')
fittle	food
frizoggled	freezing cold
gain	handy, skilful
got a nark on	annoyed (also **got a monk on, got a bag on**)
jed	dead (hence **jeth**, 'death')
lief	as soon as

mash	to brew (eg **the tea's mashing in t' pot**)
noggin	a thick piece (usually of bread)
pail	to beat (**I'll gi im a good pailin' when e comes whum**)
peg it	run away
pikelet	(two syllables: 'pike-let') crumpet
pither	potter about aimlessly
playing t'wag	playing truant
potch	forestall
reesty	(second syllable rhymes with 'sea') rancid (of fat, butter or cheese)
saft	silly, daft (so a **pack o' saftness** is a load of nonsense)
shommock	walk with a shuffling gait
skraze	graze, scratch
starving	cold (not 'hungry')
suck	sweets, candy
tacky-bonk	pit mound, slag heap (see **bonk**)
taff	to steal (perhaps from **Taff**, a nickname for a Welshman)
tararabit	(pronounced 'tara a bit') goodbye
weld	to hit someone
welly	nearly (eg **I was welly clemmed to jeth**)
wench	a girl (not derogatory, and used by both men and women)
wozzer	Birmingham term for someone from the Black Country
yawp	bawl; shout; cry loudly
zowk	yelp; cry out

East Midlands & Yorkshire

The East Midlands is made up of the counties of Nottinghamshire and Derbyshire, centred on the cities of Derby and Nottingham, and sometimes includes Leicestershire as well. Further north is the large county of Yorkshire, containing the cities of York, Sheffield and Leeds.

Combined, this is a very large region, and so of course there's a good deal of variation in speech patterns. The accents of Leeds and neighbouring Bradford are slightly different from that of Sheffield. The rural accents are different again – people from the hilly Dale country or the coastal areas have their own subtle speech variations, which reflect the isolation of smaller towns and villages.

Ah not arr

The first thing most people notice about the accents of Yorkshire and the East Midlands is the vowels. Words like 'pass' or 'grass' rhyme with 'gas', rather than with 'farce', and 'water' may rhyme with 'batter'. The *u* in words like 'duck' or 'luck' is pronounced like the *u* in 'put'.

BRASS IN POCKET

A famous Yorkshire mantra is **where there's muck there's brass**, meaning 'wherever there's dirt, there's money to be made' – a reference to the coal mines and factories that (in the past) thrived across the region. The correct northern pronunciations of the *u* (oo) and *a* (as in 'gas') sounds are essential. Say it with a southern accent and the locals may think you're a bit **nesh**.

"GEN BACKWORD
– GO BACK ON ONE'S WORD"

As in London and the southeast, *h* is generally not pronounced at the beginning of a word, so that Yorkshire people will talk about going to 'Ebden Bridge' or 'Arrogate' instead of Hebden Bridge and Harrogate. (In fact, the latter is often pronounced 'arragut'.) You'll hear Yorkshire folk dropping the word 'the' and using instead a short *t* sound, so that the expression 'I put the baby in the car' might sound like 'Ah put babby int car'. The letter *t* often turns into a *k*, so that 'little' and 'bottle' are pronounced 'lickle' and 'bockle' in some areas.

The Yorkshire habit of using **thee** and **thou** (usually pronounced 'tha' as in **Dost tha want some snap?** meaning 'Would you like some food?') can be found elsewhere in northern England. In other English-speaking countries thee and thou might seem quaintly biblical, but they're actually just a relic of earlier forms of English, in which 'you' was formal and 'thou' informal (like *tu* and *vous* in French).

East Midlands & Yorkshire words

As in many other regions, there's a wealth of dialect vocabulary in the East Midlands and Yorkshire. Some of the more common expressions are listed below.

allus	always
any road	anyway (also sometimes said **any road up**)
atta	are you (from 'art thou')
aye	yes
beck	small stream
bonny	fat, plump (not, as in northeast England and Scotland, 'attractive' – avoid saying 'Oh, you look so bonny in that dress' in Yorkshire!)

breadcake	bread roll
butty	sandwich
cack-handed	left-handed (or clumsy)
chab/chabby/ chavvy	child, baby
coursey	pavement (ie 'sidewalk' or 'footpath beside a road' in other countries)
dale	valley
gen	gave (the *g* pronounced as in 'get')
gen backword	go back on one's word (**He said he'd be there at the pub but he gen backword and never arrived**)
gennel/ginnel	alleyway; narrow path; passage between houses
give over	(pronounced 'gee owa') stop it; be quiet
gob	mouth
hacky	dirty
happen	maybe (**Happen it'll rain tomorrow**)

LOVE A DUCK

The term **love** is widely used in the East Midlands and Yorkshire. Don't get the wrong idea if you ask a Yorkshireman the time and he responds, 'Half-twelve, love'. Said to a woman, it's the equivalent of 'dear' or some other innocuous term. Said to a man, it's like 'pal', 'mate' or 'buddy'. **Duck** is used in a similar way, but is more usually (though not exclusively) addressed to women.

lak	play (eg **Yon lad were lakin' in t'ginnel** – 'That boy was playing in the alleyway')
lass	girl; woman
lugs	ears
manky	dirty
mardy	grumpy
neb	nose
nebbin/nebby	nosy
nesh	soft, weak
nowt	nothing
owt	something; anything
right	very (**It's right cold today**)
selt	past tense of 'sell' (**I selt my car yesterday**)
semt/sempt	past tense of 'seem' (eg **The baby was ill in the morning but semt all right by dinner time**) (**Selt** and **semt** are common in Derbyshire, but less so in Yorkshire)
siling down	raining heavily
sithee	See you (ie 'Goodbye')
Sithee?	Do you see? (ie 'Do you understand?')
skinny	tight-fisted, mean
skrike	cry
sock on	fast asleep
starving	cold

Northwest England

Lying between North Wales, the West Midlands and the Scottish border, with the coast of the Irish Sea on one side and the Pennine Hills on the other, is the northwest part of England. It includes the counties of Lancashire and Cumbria, the famous cities of Manchester, Liverpool and Carlisle, and the great countryside of the Lake District.

Speaking Manc like a native

To the untrained ear, the accent and dialect of the rural areas of the northwest can sound similar to those of Yorkshire, County Durham and Northumberland, on the other side of the Pennines. Certainly, many of the vowel sounds are the same, such as the short *a* – 'path', 'grass' and 'fast' have the same vowel sound as 'mat'. The *oo* in 'book', too, is pronounced in both areas rather like the *u* in 'chute'.

But don't let these similarities fool you. If you get a Lancastrian confused with someone from Yorkshire you could be in trouble: the rivalry between these counties goes back at least to the Wars of the Roses in the 15th century.

Cumbria is often said to be England's most beautiful county, thanks to its lakes and mountains and the lack of any large towns or cities. Although in previous centuries this was a major slate-working region, its rugged terrain and remoteness has helped preserve some speech forms from much earlier times. For example, the words **thee** and **thy** ('you' and 'your') are still used. Another is **dost** or **dust**, meaning 'do you?' as in **Dust come frae Ambleside?** (Do you come from Ambleside?).

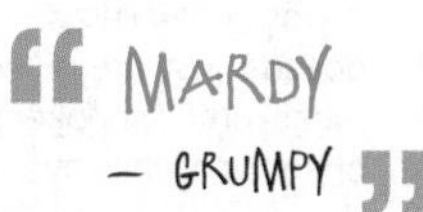

Just to the south of Cumbria and the Lake District is Lancashire. The broad Lancashire dialect has the vowel sounds outlined earlier, along with features such as pronouncing 'asking' like 'aksin', 'bowls' as 'bohwels', 'water' as 'watter', 'wash' as 'wesh' and 'wrong' as 'rang'.

The biggest city in Lancashire (although these days it's a metropolitan area in its own right) is Manchester, and it's home to a very distinct dialect known (like the inhabitants) as **Mancunian**, or simply **Manc**. The best way to get an idea of the Manc accent is to watch a few episodes of the long-running TV soap opera *Coronation Street*, which is set in Manchester.

Not far from Manchester is Liverpool, home of the most distinct accent in the Northwest, and one of the most distinct accents in the whole of Britain. Liverpool's dialect is known as **Scouse** and **Liverpudlians** are known as **Scousers** (the name is said to derive from **lobscouse** – a mutton stew – which itself is almost certainly a nativised form of the German dish *Labskaus*). Scouse has been heavily influenced by Irish English, since so many Irish immigrants have settled in the city. Its distinctive features include replacing *th* at the start of words like 'those', 'things' and 'there' with the consonants *t* or *d*, so a sentence sounding like 'What are dose tings dere?' isn't unusual. And *t* itself can often sound like *s* in Scouse, so that 'what' can sound like 'woss'.

Some words from standard English have been combined, most famously **gis**, from 'give us', meaning 'give me' (eg **Gis a job**). The *k* sound in 'back' gets a guttural *ch* pronunciation, winding

WAIT A WHILE

A word of warning – watch out for the Yorkshire **while**. It doesn't just mean 'while' in the usual sense, it can also mean 'until': shopkeepers, for example, will tell you they're open 'nine while five'.

TASTY!

Don't be surprised if someone asks you if you'd like a **shag** in Cumbria – it's local dialect for a sandwich.

up like German 'Bach'. And 'fur' and 'fair' often sound alike in Liverpool – but just to confuse the issue, sometimes Scouse 'fair' sounds like 'fur' (to rhyme with 'stir') and sometimes 'fur' sounds like 'fair' (to rhyme with 'stair').

Northwest words

Here's a very small section of words from the northwest:

bally-wart	stomach ache
barmcake	bread roll (sometimes shortened to **barm**)
beawnt	going to
brid	a child (from 'bird')
camp	chat
chuck	term of endearment (as in the greeting **Ey up chuck**)
cob on	annoyed (**E's getten a cob on**, meaning 'He's annoyed')
collops	lots of
estin	dustbin
ey lads ey	reality, basics (eg **When it comes to ey lads ey**, meaning 'In reality')
fain	glad
fratch	argue

> “A'M POWND T'DEEATH
>
> — STRESSED OUT”

frimbles	nervous, uncertain
giggle-gaggle	passage between houses
ginnel	see **giggle-gaggle**
hoo	she
jannock	reasonably good
keawer	sit
Lanky	Lancashire, or an inhabitant of that county
lish	agile; fit
mardy	grumpy; moody
moggy	in West Lancashire, a mouse rather than a cat!
moither	annoy
nazzy	bad-tempered
po fagged	exhausted
pownd	stressed (**A'm pownd t'deeath**)
shive	slice of bread
sken	to look
sneck	nose
tara	goodbye
utch	to move
wick	quick; agile; heaving with (**Wick wi' mice**)

Northeast England

Northeast England consists mainly of County Durham and Northumberland. We're now in the territory of the **Geordies** and the **Makems**, the natives of the cities of Newcastle-upon-Tyne and Sunderland, a great urban area known collectively as Tyneside. The Geordie dialect spoken in the northeast is said to be among the most difficult to understand in Britain.

To some outsiders the Geordie accent sounds similar to a Scottish accent – and there is a direct influence, as Newcastle is close to the border and throughout history has attracted Scottish immigrants. However, in many instances, visitors from overseas don't realise that local people are speaking English and think it's Russian, say, or Danish. In fact, Danish visitors to Newcastle often seem to have an easier time understanding Geordie than some native English-speakers; the strong Scandinavian influence in Tyneside has persisted since the days of the Vikings.

Don't let this worry you! If you look blank when a Geordie says **How pet, gannin' doon toon wi' wuh?** he or she will probably repeat it as 'Hello mate, do you want to go into town with us?'

" CHAMPION
– GREAT, TERRIFIC "

Tak & waak

A key feature of the Geordie accent is the pronunciation of vowels. The *o* sound often becomes *ee*, so that 'no' and 'do' are pronounced 'nee' and 'dee'. The word 'take' becomes 'tak', 'make' becomes 'mak', while 'all' becomes 'al' or 'aa', and 'walk' becomes 'waak'. Similarly, the word 'know' is 'naa', 'stone' is 'steeyen', 'shirt' is 'shawt', 'cold' is 'caad' and 'work' is 'wark' – almost like the pronunciation of 'walk' in standard English.

WHY 'GEORDIE' & 'MAKEM'?

No one is sure why the inhabitants of Newcastle-upon-Tyne are called **Geordies**. Some say it's a reference to 'Mad' King George III (**Geordie** is a diminutive of 'George') and by extension any unpredictable or undesirable person.

An inhabitant of Sunderland, the city just across the River Tyne from Newcastle, is called a **Makem** (the first syllable rhymes with 'pack'). The word is said to originate from a reference to the shipbuilding industry – once a major Tyneside employer: 'We make them and take them' (ie, we make them in the shipyard then take them down the river) which would be pronounced **we mak em and tak em**.

The word 'out' is 'oot', and a 'house' is 'hoose'; note that there's no *h*-dropping in Newcastle. In fact, sometimes an *h* is added to words such as 'away' (meaning 'let's go'), giving the classic Geordie call to arms: **Haway the lads!**

In parts of Northumberland people may be heard using the 'Northumbrian burr', a throaty *r* sound just like the one in German in words such as *braun*, produced in the back of the mouth. Also, often the sound *ow* comes out as *oo*: Newcastle brown ale, the city's iconic beverage, for example, is called Newcastle Broon.

Northeast words

One of the features of the Geordie dialect is adding the word **like** to the end of sentences, usually for emphasis: **He's a canny snooker player like.**

There are many other oddities, but the following will give you some basics:

aye yes (hence the classic Geordie phrase **way aye** – 'why yes', meaning 'absolutely')

bairn child; baby

canny clever; good; crafty; enjoyable (an all-purpose term of approval – a particular pub in Northumberland displays this sign: **Canny Ale, Canny Food, Canny Crack**)

champion great, terrific

chin break (**Sorry mam, I chinned a plate**)

clarts mud (**Me clobber's aal clarty** – 'My clothes are all dirty')

divvent don't, doesn't (**Divvent dee that!** meaning 'Don't do that!')

gadgie an old man, or sometimes an old woman

gan go (**Let's gan to the pub**)

geet very (**Wor lass is geet bonny** – 'My wife's very pretty')

glair/glaur mud

glaky slow-witted

WHAT'S THE CRACK?

In the northeast, the word **crack** has a varied job description. For example, **What's the crack?** means 'What's happening?' but **good crack** means 'a good time'. An answer to 'Why are you doing it?' could be **For the crack** (ie 'for the fun'). The word can also mean simply 'talk', 'chat' or 'gossip'.

The word crack is widely used in other parts of Britain and in Ireland (where it's spelt 'craic').

hadaway	go away; also an expression of disbelief
hinny	term of endearment, like 'honey'
howay/haway	away; let's go; also an expression of disbelief (**Howay man, ah divvent believe that like!**)
hoy	to throw (**Hoy it oot the winda!** – 'Throw it out of the window!')
hyem	home
lass	girl or young woman; **wor lass** (my lass) means 'my wife'
man	term of address for use with men, women and even small children: **Put aal your toys away Darren man**
marrer	(work)mate
mortal	drunk
nettie	toilet
pallatic	drunk (from 'paralytic')
pickle	a small quantity (**Gi'us a pickle mair** – 'Give me a bit more')
poke	bag
scutty	scruffy

> 'HOY IT OOT THE WINDA!'
> – 'THROW IT OUT THE WINDOW!'

Wales

Wales is a separate country (called a **principality**) within Britain that came under the control of the English king Edward I in the 12th century, and was formally united with England in 1535. Despite several centuries of enforced anglicisation, Welsh - a Celtic language, totally different from English - has managed to survive, and since the 1980s has been enjoying a renaissance.

Many Welsh people - particularly in the north and west of the country - speak Welsh as a first language and English as a second language. In the south, English is generally the first language, but most people speak or understand some Welsh, and Welsh is a compulsory subject in schools. Consequently, the English spoken in Wales is heavily influenced by the Welsh accent and vocabulary.

That 'sing-song' sound

Features of the Welsh accent when speaking English include the frequent dropping of the *h* sound and a tendency to pronounce *f* more like a *v*, so that the English city of Hereford (just over the border from Wales) would be pronounced 'Erevod' (pronounced as three syllables: 'e-re-vod'). You may also hear Welsh people 'doubling' the consonants in English words. The word 'patter' for example comes out more like 'pat-ter'. The same thing happens with words like 'cottage', 'adding', 'rubber' or 'village'.

Another very noticeable feature of Welsh English is its 'sing-song' intonation, which has been carried over from the Welsh language.

Welsh words

Some of the vocabulary used in Wales, and the way it's used, also owes its origin to the Welsh language. For example, a Welsh speaker might say **Look at that trousers** - because the word for 'trousers' is singular in Welsh. Another common feature in Welsh English is the use of **there's** - Welsh people may say **There's lovely!** or **There's cosy!** instead of 'That's lovely!' or 'How cosy!'

" LONK
– HUNGRY "

Listen out too for the unique Welsh use of the word **now**, as in **I'll be there now** (from the Welsh phrase *Bydda i 'na nawr*, pronounced 'beetha i na nawr'). 'Now' doesn't always mean 'this very moment'; it can also mean 'a short time in the future', so **I'll be there now** means 'I'll be there in a few minutes'. Similarly, Welsh people speaking English use the word 'to' in a way speakers of standard English may find unusual. For example, **Where's my wallet to?** means 'Where's my wallet?'

The English spoken in Wales also makes great use of the handy catch-all phrase **is it?** at the end of a sentence, regardless of the verb that went before it. So you might hear, for example, **Wales are playing England at rugby tomorrow, is it?** as opposed to 'Wales are playing England at rugby tomorrow, are they?' **Is it?** is most commonly used, however, as an all-purpose response meaning something like 'Oh, right', or 'Did you?' as in:

Jack: **We went to Newport yesterday.**

Dai: **Is it?**

Below is a list of words commonly used in Welsh English. Many are Welsh words simply carried over from the Welsh language to English, either in their original form or with some anglicisation along the way:

bach (pronounced like 'Bach' the composer, but with the *a* as in 'bag'; from the Welsh for 'small') child; a term of friendship or endearment (**All right, bach?** is the equivalent of 'All right, mate?)

bad ill, unwell (also used in many other dialects in England)

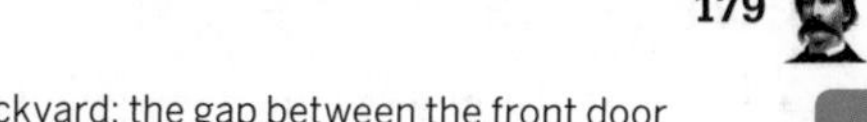

bailey	backyard; the gap between the front door and the gate of a house
butty	friend (possibly the origin of the US term 'buddy')
cammit	crooked (from Welsh *cam*, meaning 'crooked')
cwm	valley (pronounced 'coom', but with the vowel not as long as in English 'coombe')
lairy	weary
lonk	hungry
lose	miss (as in **he lost the bus**)
off	hostile, angry
petty	toilet
pilm	dust
pursy/putsy	easy
simple	ill, unwell
sorty	proud
tidy	can mean 'good-looking' (as in **She's a tidy girl**), 'well done' (**a tidy job**), 'properly' (as in **Sing it again, but this time do it tidy**) or 'decent' (**He's a tidy sort of bloke**)
top room	sitting room, best room, parlour
trwstan	clumsy (pronounced 'troostan')
tump	hill, mound (from Welsh *twmp*, meaning 'hill')
twp	simple, slow-witted (pronounced 'toop' – see pronunciation of **cwm**)

As well as borrowing Welsh words and/or usage, Welsh English has a tendency to follow Welsh grammar, meaning word order is sometimes changed to emphasise a particular aspect of the sentence. So **Hurt she was** brings the injury into sharper focus, and **Terrible they played** or **Awful I thought it sounded** give the 'terribleness' and 'awfulness' centre stage.

Scotland

Forming the northern part of Britain, Scotland is another separate country within the United Kingdom. Devolution (partial autonomy) came to Scotland in 1999 with the opening of the nation's own parliament in Edinburgh, after 300 years of rule from London. Even before this, Scotland stood apart from England by maintaining its own legal system, educational system, cultural traditions and – of course – languages.

In the same way that the Welsh language influenced the English spoken in Wales, so the English dialects spoken in Scotland have been influenced by its two indigenous languages – **Scottish Gaelic** (pronounced *gah*·lik), often known as **Highland Scots**, and **Lallans** or **Lowland Scots**. The names reflect the areas where they are or were spoken – the Highlands is essentially the north and west of Scotland. They also give the erroneous impression that Highland Scots and Lowland Scots are two variants of the same language, when they are in fact completely unrelated. Scottish Gaelic is a Celtic tongue related to Welsh; Lallans is a Germanic language closely related to English, with influences from Old Norse

In the areas where English has been spoken for a long time – the Borders region in the south of Scotland, the east coast between Perth and Aberdeen, and the so-called Central Belt containing Glasgow and Edinburgh and the surrounding areas – distinct versions of English have developed which can be difficult for outsiders to penetrate.

In contrast, in the Highlands and in Scotland's numerous islands the widespread use of English is a relatively recent development, and so the English spoken in these areas does not contain many dialect terms.

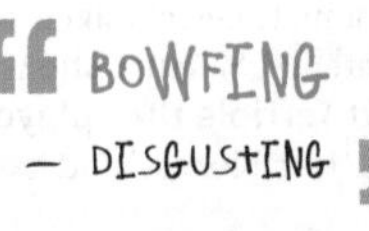

Roll those rrrs

One of the most obvious features of the Scottish accent is the use of the trilled *r* in words like 'car', 'four', 'barn' and 'first' (used in an emphasised form by cartoon characters Scrooge McDuck and Willy the janitor from *The Simpsons*). You'll also hear the guttural *ch* sound (as in 'Bach') used quite a bit by Scots, in words like **loch** or the exclamation **Och!**

Also, in Scottish English the vowel sounds in many words are different: the word 'home' is pronounced 'hame', 'stone' is 'stane', 'long' is 'lang', 'head' is 'heed' and 'dead' is pronounced 'deed'. 'House' is 'hoose', 'down' is 'doon' and 'out' is 'oot'.

Scottish words

Some grammatical constructions you may hear in Scottish English may appear unusual. For example:

My hair needs washed
My hair needs washing

I might could go tomorrow
I might be able to go tomorrow

There it's!
There it is!

That cup is mines
That cup is mine

Other constructions include the use of **will I** where 'shall I' would be used in standard English (eg **Will I put this bread in a bag for you?**) and **that's me** meaning 'I'm finished'. **I'm away** means 'I'm leaving now'. **Outwith** means 'outside'.

For the word 'today' some Scots tend to say **the day** (which is, incidentally, the derivation of the word in standard English) and for 'tomorrow', **the morn. The morn's morn** is 'tomorrow morning'.

Scottish English also makes a distinction between the singular and plural forms of 'you'. The singular is the recognisable **you**; the plural is **youse** (pronounced 'yooz') – eg **Are youse kids coming doon?** (Several other dialects of English, in Britain and beyond, also make this distinction.)

Of the urban dialects, those from Glasgow and Edinburgh are perhaps the best known. The pronunciation and intonation differences between them are fairly minor.

Below is a taster of some of the words and phrases you may come across. Some words are Gaelic or Lallans in origin, either used in their original form in Scottish English, or with anglicised spelling.

ay	(pronounced 'eye') yes
aye	(pronounced 'eye') always – so a letter may be signed **Aye yours, Fiona**)
barry	excellent, as in **That match was pure barry**
ben	hill or mountain (from Gaelic **beinn**)
blether	blather, drivel, waffle
bogging	disgusting; unpleasant; ugly (pronounced 'boggin')
bowfing	disgusting; unpleasant; ugly (pronounced 'bowfin')
braw	great, good
burn	stream, brook
cannae	cannot
cauld	cold
ceilidh	party, dance, get-together (Gaelic for 'gathering', pronounced 'kaylee')
cheg	steal

clan	family; group of related families (from Gaelic *clann*, meaning 'children')
clanjamfrie/ clamjamfry	a crowd; odds and ends
clarty	dirty; muddy
clinging	disgusting; unpleasant; ugly (pronounced 'clingin')
crabbit	bad-tempered, sullen
dinnae	do not
dram	a measure of spirits (eg **Will you stop by for a dram of whisky?**)
dreich	miserable, wet, gloomy (of weather)
gallus	mischievous
gey	very (**It's gey cauld today**)
glaikit	slow-witted
glen	valley (from Gaelic *gleann*)
gnash	hurry (**C'mon youse, gnash!**)
gowk	idiot, fool (literally 'cuckoo')
greet	cry (**Dinnae greet, it's only a skelf!** – 'Don't cry, it's only a splinter!')
haar	thick, damp mist coming in off the sea
Haud yer whisht!	Be quiet!
haver	to chatter aimlessly or foolishly, to waffle
hen	term of endearment (towards women); when used by men discussing women, it means 'babe' or 'chick' (eg 'Andrew, you said we'd meet a couple of hens tonight')
Jings!	an exclamation along the lines of 'Good heavens!'

ken	know
loch	lake
loup	to run; to jump
lum	chimney
minging	disgusting; unpleasant; ugly (pronounced 'mingin')
muckle/mickle	big
nip	a measure of spirits (smaller than a **dram**)
nyaff	idiot
pech	pant, puff (often after climbing a **ben**)

IMPENETRABLE AS GRANITE

Any language difficulties you may have in Glasgow or Edinburgh are nothing compared to those associated with the Aberdeen dialect. The Scandinavian influence is stronger in Aberdeen (nicknamed the Granite City) than anywhere else in Scotland, as boats from Norway and Denmark call in here, and it's sometimes hard to tell apart the speech of these tourists and that of the Aberdonian locals using their broadest vernacular. A common greeting is **Fit like?** ('How are you?'), which can be answered **Tyaavin awa**, meaning 'I'm fine' or **Gweed** ('Good'). If a tourist is asked **Far d'ye bide?** ('Where do you live?') and the answer's Australia, a local might say **Ah hine awa** ('Ah, far away'). A few other local words are **foggie-bummers** (bumblebees) and **horny-gollochs** (earwigs). Foreigners are **fremmit** and **dubs** is mud.

“AULD REEKIE

– NICKNAME FOR EDINBURGH (OLD SMOKY)”

radge	slightly deranged person (**Ignore him, he's a radge**); exciting or out of the ordinary (**He's totally radge, that guy**)
rare	great, good
reek	smoke (hence **Auld Reekie** – 'Old Smoky' – the nickname for Edinburgh)
Sassenach	slightly insulting term for an English person (from the Gaelic word for 'Saxon'), although sometimes applied to any non-Highlander or non-Gaelic-speaking Scot
scaff	tramp; badly dressed person
scunnered	disgusted, repelled
shan	bad; awful; unkind
shoogle	shake
Slàinte!	Cheers! (pronounced 'sland-ge')
stoor	dust
stoorie	hurry; run away
strath	valley (from Gaelic *srath*)
swally	(alcoholic) drink
Teuchter	a Highlander (mocking)
yon	that, like old English term 'yonder' (eg **Do you ken yon laddie?** – 'Do you know that boy over there?')

REGIONAL
LANGUAGES

REGIONAL LANGUAGES

Welsh

Although Welsh people speak English, a few words of Welsh (**Cymraeg**, pronounced kuhm·*raig*) will be appreciated by locals. Welsh is the strongest of the Celtic languages, both in terms of number of speakers (around 300,000) and its place in society. However, a 2012 report found that the number of fluent Welsh speakers is falling by about 3000 a year as people die or move from Wales.

The language belongs to the Celtic branch of the Indo-European family – it's closely related to Breton and Cornish, and more distantly to Irish, Scottish and Manx. At one time it was spoken throughout the island of Britain south of a line between modern Glasgow and Edinburgh, but was gradually pushed westwards by the invading Angles and Saxons in the 5th century.

Up until the Industrial Revolution, most Welsh people spoke only Welsh, but by the early modern period Welsh had lost its status as an official language. In 1900 some 50 per cent still spoke Welsh; by 1961, however, only 26 per cent were Welsh-speaking and there was general alarm that the language would disappear. The following year Saunders Lewis's BBC radio lecture 'The Fate of the Language' (*Tynged yr Iaith*, pronounced *tuhng*·ed uhr yaith) led to the creation of the Welsh Language Society (*Cymdeithas yr Iaith Gymraeg*, pronounced kuhm·*day*·thas uhr yaith guhm·*raig*), a protest movement in support of the language. Its civil disobedience campaigns succeeded in winning equal recognition for Welsh in one domain of society after another.

Pronunciation

Stress in Welsh almost always falls on the penultimate syllable of a word. In the pronunciation guides, words are divided into syllables by a dot and stressed syllables are italicised.

Vowel sounds

Symbol	English equivalent	Welsh example	Transliteration
a	**a**ct	c**a**m	k**a**m
ah	f**a**ther	d**a**	d**ah**
ai	**ai**sle	s**ai**th	s**ai**th
ay	h**ay**	pe**i**nt	p**ay**nt
e	p**e**n	h**e**t	h**e**t
ee	s**ee**	d**y**n	d**ee**n
eh	th**ere**	h**e**n	h**eh**n
ew	f**ew**	d**uw**	d**ew**
i	s**i**n	c**y**n	k**i**n
o	h**o**t	ff**o**n	f**o**n
oh	**oh**	s**ô**n	s**oh**n
oo	f**oo**l	m**w**g	m**oo**g
ow	n**ow**	n**aw**	n**ow**
oy	b**oy**	c**oe**s	k**oy**s
u	p**u**t	c**w**m	k**u**m
uh	**a**go	**y**n	**uh**n

Consonant sounds

Symbol	English equivalent	Welsh example	Transliteration
b	**b**ox	**b**ryd	**b**reed
d	**d**og	**d**yn	**d**een
dh	**th**is	**dd**oe	**dh**oy
f	**f**un	**ff**ordd	**f**ohrdh
g	**g**ame	**g**lan	**g**lan
h	**h**at	**h**af	**h**ahv
hl	h and l together with a puff of air	**ll**yn	**hl**in
hr	h and r together with a puff of air	**rh**iw	**hr**ew
j	**j**ump	**j**am	**j**am
k	**c**at	**c**i	**k**ee
kh	lo**ch**	ba**ch**	ba**kh**
l	**l**augh	**l**awnt	**l**ownt
m	**m**eal	**m**awr	**m**owr
n	**n**aughty	**n**os	**n**ohs
ng	si**ng**	a**ng**en	a**ng**·en
p	**p**rice	**p**en	**p**en
r	**r**ed (trilled)	ca**r**w	ka·**r**oo
s	**s**in	**s**ant	**s**ant
sh	**sh**ell	**si**op	**sh**op
t	**t**ickle	**t**iwn	**t**eewn
th	**th**ick	ca**th**	ka**th**
v	**v**at	**f**yny	**v**uh·nee
w	**w**ee	ch**w**erw	kh**w**e·roo
y	**y**es	**i**awn	**y**own

Numbers

0	**dim**	dim
1	**un**	een
2	**dau/dwy** (m/f)	dai/*doo*·ee
3	**tri/tair** (m/f)	tree/tair
4	**pedwar/pedair** (m/f)	*ped*·wahr/*pe*·dair
5	**pump**	pimp
6	**chwech**	khwehkh
7	**saith**	saith
8	**wyth**	*oo*·ith
9	**naw**	now
10	**deg**	dehg

Time & dates

Days

Monday	**Dydd Llun** (m)	deedh hleen
Tuesday	**Dydd Mawrth** (m)	deedh mowrth
Wednesday	**Dydd Mercher** (m)	deedh *mehr*·kher
Thursday	**Dydd Iau** (m)	deedh yai
Friday	**Dydd Gwener** (m)	deedh *gwe*·ner
Saturday	**Dydd Sadwrn** (m)	deedh *sa*·doorn
Sunday	**Dydd Sul** (m)	deedh seel

“PEN-BLWYDD HAPUS!

— HAPPY BIRTHDAY”

HAPPY DAYS

Happy Birthday! **Pen-Blwydd Hapus!**	pen·*bloo*·idh *ha*·pis
Happy Christmas! **Nadolig Llawen!**	na·*do*·lig *hlow*·en
Happy New Year! **Blwyddyn Newydd Da!**	*bloo*·idh·in *neh*·widh dhah

Months

Half of the names of the months in Welsh were originally borrowed from Latin, and half (those that have literal translations below) are Welsh.

January	**Mis Ionawr** (m)	mees *yoh*·nowr
February	**Mis Chwefror** (m)	mees *khwev*·ror
March	**Mis Mawrth** (m)	mees mowrth
April	**Mis Ebrill** (m)	mees *eb*·rihl
May	**Mis Mai** (m)	mees mai
June	**Mis Mehefin** (m) (lit: middle-of-summer)	mees me·*he*·vin
July	**Mis Gorffennaf** (m) (lit: end-of-summer)	mees gor·*fe*·nav
August	**Mis Awst** (m)	mees owst
September	**Mis Medi** (m) (lit: reaping)	mees *me*·di
October	**Mis Hydref** (m) (lit: stag-roaring; ie rutting season)	mees *huhd*·rev
November	**Mis Tachwedd** (m) (lit: slaughter)	mees *takh*·wedh
December	**Mis Rhagfyr** (m) (lit: before-short; ie before the shortest day)	mees *hrag*·veer

Time

minute	**munud** (f)	*mi*·nid
hour	**awr** (f)	owr
week	**wythnos** (f) (lit: eight-nights)	oo·*ith*·nos
month	**mis** (m)	mees
today	**heddiw**	*hedh*·yoo
tomorrow	**yfory**	uh·*voh*·ree

Hellos & goodbyes

Hello
Sut mae sit mai

Good morning
Bore da *boh*·re dah

Good afternoon
Prynhawn da *prin*·hown dah

Good evening
Noswaith dda *nos*·waith dhah

Goodnight
Nos da nohs dah

See you (later)
Wela i chi (wedyn) *we*·la ee khee (*we*·din)

How are you?
Sut ydych chi? sit *uh*·dikh khee

(Very) well
Da (iawn) dah (yown)

Goodbye
Hwyl fawr *hoo*·il vowr

Excuse me
Esgusodwch fi *es*·gi·so·dookh vee

May I?
Ga i? gah ee

Do you mind?
Oes ots gyda chi? oys ots *gi*·da khee

Sorry
Mae'n ddrwg gen i main dhroog gen ee

Please
Os gwelwch yn dda os *gwe*·lookh uhn dhah

Thank you (very much)
Diolch (yn fawr iawn) dyolkh (uhn vowr yown)

You're welcome
Croeso *kroy*·so

Don't mention it
Peidiwch â sôn *pay*·dyookh a sohn

I don't know
Wn i ddim oon ee dhim

Yes/No
Ie/Nage yeh/*nah*·geh

WELL-WISHING

Cheers!
Iechyd Da! *ye*·khid dah

Get well soon!
Brysiwch wella! *bruh*·shookh *we*·hla

Bless you! (for sneezing)
Bendith! *ben*·dith

What a pity!
Dyna drueni! *duh*·na dree·*eh*·ni

Bon voyage!
Siwrnai dda! *shoor*·ne dhah

Good luck!
Pob lwc! pob luk

Hope it goes well!
Pob hwyl! pob *hoo*·il

"WELA I CHI WEDYN — SEE YOU LATER"

Interests

What do you like doing?

Beth ydych chi'n hoffi wneud? — beth *uh*·dikh kheen *ho*·fee w·*naid*

I like (swimming) and (going to the cinema)

Dw i'n hoffi (nofio) a (mynd i'r sinema) — doo een *ho*·fee (*nov*·yo) a (mind eer *si*·ne·ma)

I don't like (cooking)

Dw i ddim yn hoffi (coginio) — doo ee dhim uhn *ho*·fee (ko·*gin*·yo)

Do you like (sport)?

Ydych chi'n hoffi (chwaraeon)? — *uh*·dikh kheen *ho*·fee (khwah·*ray*·on)

Yes, very much

Ydw, yn fawr iawn — uh·*doo* uhn vowr yown

No, not at all

Nac ydw, dim o gwbl — nak uh·*doo* dim o *gu*·bul

Going out

What are you doing this evening?

Beth ydych chi'n wneud heno? — beth *uh*·dikh kheen w·*naid he*·no

Nothing special

Dim byd arbennig — dim beed ar·*be*·nig

Would you like to go out somewhere?

Hoffech chi fynd allan i rywle? — *ho*·fekh khee vind *a*·hlan ee *rew*·le

Would you like to go for a drink/meal?	
Hoffech chi fynd allan am ddiod/bryd o fwyd?	*ho*·fekh khee vind *a*·hlan am *dhee*·od/breed o *voo*·id
I'll buy	
Fe dala i	veh *da*·la ee
Do you feel like (going for a swim)?	
Oes awydd (mynd i nofio) arnoch chi?	oys *ow*·idh (mind ee *nov*·yo) *ar*·nokh khee
Yes, that'd be lovely	
Hoffwn, byddai hynny'n hyfryd	*ho*·foon *buh*·dhai *huh*·neen *huh*·vrid

"BYDDAI HYNNY'N HYFRYD – THAT WOULD BE LOVELY"

Yes, where to?	
Hoffwn. Ble awn ni?	*ho*·foon bleh own nee
Yes, that'd be great	
Oes, byddai hynny'n wych	oys *buh*·dhai *huh*·neen weekh
OK	
Iawn	yown
No, I'm afraid I can't	
Alla i ddim, mae arna i ofn	*a*·hla ee dhim mai *ar*·na ee *o*·vuhn
I'm sorry, I can't	
Mae'n ddrwg gen i, alla i ddim	main dhroog gen ee *a*·hla ee dhim
Not at the moment, thanks	
Ddim ar hyn o bryd, diolch	dhim ahr hin o breed dyolkh

What about tomorrow?
Beth am yfory? beth am uh·*voh*·ree

I feel like going to...
Mae gen i awydd mynd i... mai gen ee *ow*·idh mind ee...

Arranging to meet

What time shall we meet?
Am faint o'r gloch wnawn ni gyfarfod? am vaint ohr glohkh w·*nown* nee guh·*var*·vod

Where shall we meet?
Ble wnawn ni gyfarfod? bleh w·*nown* nee guh·*var*·vod

Let's meet at (eight o'clock) in St Mary Street
Beth am gyfarfod am (wyth o'r gloch) yn Heol y Santes Fair beth am guh·*var*·vod am (*oo*·ith ohr glohkh) uhn *hay*·ol uh *san*·tes vair

OK, I'll see you then
Iawn, wela i chi bryd hynny yown *wel*·a ee khee breed *huh*·nee

Afterwards

It was nice talking to you
Roedd hi'n braf siarad â chi roydh uhn brahv *sha*·rad a khee

I have to get going now
Rhaid imi fynd nawr hraid *ee*·mee vind nowr

I had a great day/evening
Ces i ddiwrnod gwych/noson wych kehs ee *dyoor*·nod gweekh/*nos*·on weekh

Hope to see you again soon
Gobeithio eich gweld chi eto yn fuan go·*bayth*·yo aykh gweld khee *et*·ohn *vee*·an

WELSH PLACE NAMES

The town of Llanfairpwllgwyngyllgogerychwyrndrobwlll-lan-tysiliogogogoch (*hlan*·vair·poohl·*gwin*·gihl·go·gehr·uh·*khwuhrn*·*dro*·buhl·hlan·tuh·*sil*·yo·go·go·*gokh*) has legendary status as the longest place name in the UK. It translates as 'Saint Mary's Church in the hollow of the white hazel near a rapid whirlpool and the Church of St Tysilio of the red cave'.

I'll give you a call
Ffônia i chi — fo*hn*·ya ee khee

What's your number?
Beth yw eich rhif? — beth ew aykh hreev

Eating out

A table for..., please.
Bwrdd i... os gwelwch yn dda — boordh ee... os *gwe*·lookh uhn dhah

Can I see the menu, please?
Ga i weld y fwydlen, os gwelwch yn dda? — gah ee weld uh *voo*·eed·len os *gwe*·lookh uhn dhah

The bill, please
Y bil, os gwelwch yn dda — uh bil os *gwe*·lookh uhn dhah

In the pub

I'd like a (half) pint of...	**Ga i (hanner o) beint o...**	gah ee (*han*·er oh) baynt oh...
bitter	**chwerw**	*khwe*·roo
cider	**seidr**	*say*·duhr
lager	**lager**	*lah*·guhr

Scottish Gaelic

As with the Welsh, all Scots speak English, but a little effort put into learning some phrases in Scottish Gaelic (**Gàidhlig**, *gah*·lik) will be rewarded. Just keep in mind that of the roughly 60,000 people who speak Scottish Gaelic, most live in the Highlands and Islands in the west and northwest of Scotland. Increasing numbers also live in or near large urban centres such as Glasgow and Edinburgh. Outside the Highlands, though, you may get blank looks if you venture anything more complicated than a greeting in Gaelic!

Scottish Gaelic belongs to the **Goidelic** branch of Celtic. Irish (**Gaeilge**) and Manx (**Gaelg**), an extinct language from the Isle of Man, are closely related to Scottish Gaelic.

It's generally believed that Gaelic was brought to Scotland by Irish settlers some time in or before the 5th century AD. The Romans called these settlers *Scotti* (literally 'Irishmen'), which later gave rise to the country's name. By the 11th and 12th centuries, Scottish Gaelic was spoken in most parts of modern Scotland. However, from this point up to the late 19th century, Gaelic was in decline for much of the time, beginning in the Lowlands where there was most English influence and persecution. Gaelic flourished in the Highlands until the 18th century, the time of the Jacobite rebellions and wars. The dispersion forced by the Highland Clearances (*na Fuadaichean*, nuh *foo*·duh·khuhn) of the 19th century and the destruction of the Gaelic school system by the *1872 Education Act* (*Scotland*) did further damage.

Fortunately, the tide has since turned, due to efforts from the later 19th century to raise the profile of Gaelic and increase the confidence of speakers in their language and culture. A measure of security has also been granted by the UK's 2001 ratification of the European Charter for Regional or Minority Languages.

Pronunciation

Stress in Scottish Gaelic almost always falls on the first syllable of a word. Stressed syllables are italicised in the pronunciation guides.

Vowel sounds

Note that the **r** is not pronounced in the **er** sound listed below.

Symbol	English equivalent	Gaelic example	Transliteration
ah	f**a**ther	th**a**	h**ah**
ai	**ai**sle	ch**aidh**	h**ai**
aw	r**aw**	l**o**ch	l**aw**kh
e	h**e**x	b**ea**n	b**e**n
ee	s**ee**	m**i**	m**ee**
eh	h**ai**r	**ai**r	**eh**r
er	h**er**	**ao**n	**er**n
i	s**i**n	f**io**s	f**i**s
oh	**oh**	m**ò**r	m**oh**r
oo	h**oo**t	**ugh**	**oo**
ow	c**ow**	**a**nn	**ow**n
oy	b**oy**	d**ò**igh	d**oy**
uh	**a**go	ag**a**m	*ah*·k**uh**m

Consonant sounds

Symbol	English equivalent	Gaelic example	Transliteration
b	**b**ox	**b**òrd	**b**orsht
ch	**ch**eese	àite	ah·**ch**uh
d	**d**og	**d**uine	**d**er·nyuh
f	**f**un	**f**ios	**f**is
g	**g**ame	**g**orm	**g**aw·ruhm
gh	between *g* and the 'ch' in 'lo**ch**'	a **dh**à	uh **gh**ah
h	**h**at	**th**a	**h**ah
j	**j**ump	**d**ìreach	**j**ee·ruhkh
k	**c**at	**c**as	**k**as
kh	lo**ch**	a**ch**	ah**kh**
l	**l**augh	**l**itir	**l**ee·chuhr
m	**m**eal	**m**ath	**m**ah
n	**n**aughty	gla**n**	glah**n**
ng	si**ng**	lo**ng**	law**ng**k
p	**p**en	**p**ìos	**p**ees
r	like 'tt' in 'bu**tt**er' said fast	**r**uadh	**r**oo·uhgh
s	**s**in	**s**olu**s**	**s**oh·luh**s**
sh	**sh**ell	**s**ìos	**sh**ee·uhs
t	**t**ickle	**t**aigh	**t**ai
v	**v**at	à-**bh**eil	uh·**v**el
w	**w**in	**u**ill	**w**el
y	**y**es	coi**mh**ead	kaw·**y**uht

Numbers

0	**neoini**	*nyaw*·nee
1	**a h-aon**	uh hern
2	**a dhà**	uh ghah
3	**a trì**	uh tree
4	**a ceithir**	uh *keh*·hir
5	**a cóig**	uh *coh*·ik
6	**a sia**	uh *shee*·uh
7	**a seachd**	uh shahkhk
8	**a hochd**	uh hawkhk
9	**a naoi**	uh *ner*·ee
10	**a deich**	uh jehkh

Time & dates

Time

minute	**mionaid** (f)	*mi*·nuhch
hour	**uair** (f)	*oo*·uhr
week	**seachdain** (f)	*shahkh*·kuhn
month	**mìos** (m)	*mee*·uhs
today	**(an latha) an-diugh**	(uhn lah) uhn·*joo*
tomorrow	**a-màireach**	uh·*mah*·ruhkh

Days

Monday	**Diluain** (m)	jee·*loo*·uhn
Tuesday	**Dimàirt** (m)	jee·mahrshch
Wednesday	**Diciadaoin** (m)	jee·*kee*·uh·tuhn
Thursday	**Diardaoin** (m)	jee·*der*·een
Friday	**Dihaoine** (m)	jee·*hoo*·nyuh
Saturday	**Disathairne** (m)	jee·*sah*·huhr·nuh

There are two words used for 'Sunday' listed below – the first tends to be used by Catholics and Episcopalians, the second by Presbyterians.

Sunday	**Didòmhnaich** (m)	jee·*daw*·nikh
Sunday	**Latha na Sàbaid** (m)	lah nuh *sah*·pich

The word **latha** (day) is now also commonly spelled **là**. The pronunciation, lah, is the same in both cases.

Months

January	**am Faoileach**	uhm *fer*·ee·luhkh
February	**an Gearran**	uhn *gya*·ruhn
March	**am Màrt**	uhm mahrsht
April	**an Giblean**	uhn *gip*·luhn
May	**an Cèitean**	uhn *keh*·chuhn
June	**an t-Ògmhìos**	uhn *tawk*·vee·uhs
July	**an t-Iuchar**	uhn *choo*·khuhr
August	**an Lùnastal**	uhn *loo*·nuh·stuhl
September	**an t-Sultain**	uhn *tool*·tin
October	**an Dàmhair**	uhn *dah*·vuhr
November	**an t-Samhain**	uhn *tow*·in
December	**an Dùbhlachd**	uhn *doo*·luhkhk

" OIDHCHE CHALLAINN

— HOGMANAY, NEW YEAR'S EVE "

Directions

Where's the...?	**Càite a' bheil...?**	*kah*·chuh vel ...
I want to go to the...	**Tha mi ag iarraidh a dhol do...**	hah mee *gee*·uh·ree uh ghawl doh...
airport	**am port-adhair**	uhm *pawrsht*·ahr
bank	**am banca**	uhm *bahn*·kuh
church	**an eaglais**	uhn *ek*·lish
cinema	**an taigh-dhealbh**	uhn tai·*yah*·luhv
ferry	**an t-aiseag**	uhn *tah*·shuhk
hotel	**an taigh-òsta**	uhn tai·*aw*·stuh
library	**an leabharlann**	uhn *lyoh*·uhr·lown
post office	**oifis a' phuist**	*aw*·fish uh fooshch
pub	**an taigh-seinnse**	uhn tai·*shehn*·shuh
shop	**a' bhùth**	uh voo
shops	**na bhùthan**	nuh *voo*·uhn
station	**an stèisean**	uhn *steh*·shuhn
swimming pool	**an t-amar snàimh**	uhn *tah*·muhr snahv
toilet	**an taigh-beag**	uhn *tai*·bek
tourist information centre	**ionad fiosrachaidh luchd turais**	*in*·uht *fis*·ruh·khee lookhk *too*·rish
town centre	**meadhan a' bhaile**	*mee*·uhn uh *vah*·luh

HAPPY DAYS

There are plenty of occasions to celebrate in Scotland and below are Gaelic words for the major festivals. New Year's Eve, or *Oidhche Challainn* (*ai*·khuh *khah*·lin, also known in English as Hogmanay), sees friends and relatives visiting each other after the New Year has been rung in and exchanging drinks. This is commonly referred to as **first footing**.

Christmas	**Là Nollaig**	lah *naw*·lik
New Year's Day	**Là na Bliadhna Ùire**	lah nuh *blee*·uh·nuh *oo*·ruh
Hallowe'en	**Oidhche Shamhna**	*ai*·khuh *how*·nuh
May Day	**Là Bealltainn**	lah *byowl*·tin
Lammas Day	**Là Lùnastail**	lah *loo*·nuh·stuhl
First day of spring	**Là Fhèill Brighde**	lah el *bree*·juh
Easter	**a' Chàisg**	uh khahshk
St Andrew's Day	**Fèill Anndrais**	fel *own*·drish

It's...	**Tha e...**	hah eh...
here	**an seo**	uhn shaw
there	**an sin**	uhn shin
over there (near)	**thall an sin**	howl uhn shin
over there (far)	**thall an siud**	howl uhn shoot
up there	**shuas an sin**	*hoo*·uhs uhn shin
down there	**shìos an sin**	*hee*·uhs uhn shin
near (the shop)	**faisg air (a' bhùth)**	fashk ehr (uh voo)
past (the bank)	**seachad air (a' bhanca)**	*shah*·khuht ehr (uh *vahn*·kuh)

Hellos & goodbyes

Scottish Gaelic has no word for 'hello'. Instead, people greet others by asking how they are and making comments on the weather. However, expressions based on English are becoming more common.

What's your name?
Dè an t-ainm a tha ort? (inf) — jen *tah*·nuhm uh hawrsht
Dè an t-ainm a tha oirbh? (pol) — jen *tah*·nuhm uh *haw*·ruhf

How are you?
Ciamar a tha thu/ sibh? (inf/pol) — *kim*·uhr uh hah oo/ shif

Well
Tha gu math — hah goo mah

Not bad
Chan eil dona — khahn yel *daw*·nuh

Good morning
Madainn mhath — *mah*·tin vah

Good afternoon/evening
Feasgar math — *fes*·kuhr mah

Good night
Oidhche mhath — *ai*·khuh vah

It's a lovely day
Tha là brèagha ann — hah lah *bree*·uh own

It's cold today
Tha e fuar an-diugh — hah eh *foo*·uhr uhn·*joo*

It's raining
Tha an t-uisge ann — hah uhn *toosh*·kuh own

SIGNS

am Poileas	uhm *paw*·lis	Police
Ceud Mìle Fàilte	keht *mee*·luh *fahl*·chuh	A Hundred Thousand Welcomes
Fàilte gu...	*fahl*·chuh goo...	Welcome to...
Fòn	fohn	Telephone
Sràid	strahch	Street
Taigh-beag	tai bek	Toilet
Fir	feer	Men
Mnathan	muh·*nah*·huhn	Women
Taigh-tasgaidh	tai·*tah*·skee	Museum

It's snowing
Tha sneachd ann — hah snyakh own

It's misty
Tha ceò ann — hah kyoh own

Goodbye (lit: blessing with you)
Beannachd leat (sg inf) — *byah*·nuhkhk laht

Goodbye (lit: blessing with you)
Beannachd leibh (pl & sg pol) — *byah*·nuhkhk laiv

Goodbye (lit: the same to you)
Mar sin leat/leibh (inf/pol) — mahr shin laht/laiv

Who are you?
Có thusa? — koh *oo*·suh

I'm...
Is mise... — *smee*·shuh...

Thank you	**Tapadh leat** (sg inf)	*tah*·puh laht
Thank you	**Tapadh leibh** (pl & sg pol)	*tah*·puh laiv
Thanks	**Taing**	*tah*·eeng
Many thanks	**Mòran taing**	*moh*·ruhn *tah*·eeng
Please	**Mas e do thoil e** (sg inf)	mash eh duh hawl eh
Please	**Mas e ur toil e** (pl & sg pol)	mash eh oor tawl eh
You're welcome	**'S e do bheatha** (sg inf)	sheh duh *veh*·huh
You're welcome	**'S e ur beatha** (pl & sg pol)	sheh oor *beh*·huh
Excuse me	**Gabh mo leisgeul** (sg inf)	gahv muh *lesh*·kuhl
Excuse me	**Gabhaibh mo leisgeul** (pl & sg pol)	*gah*·viv muh *lesh*·kuhl
I'm sorry	**Tha mi duilich**	hah mee *doo*·likh
Come along	**Trobhad**	*troh*·uht
Let's go	**Thugainn**	*hoo*·kin
Go on	**Siubhad**	*shoo*·uht
Yuck!	**A ghia!**	uh *yee*·uh
Goodness me!	**A thiarcais fhèin!**	uh *heer*·kish hehn
Pardon me	**(Dè) b'àill leibh**	(jeh) bahl laiv
I don't mind	**Tha mi coma**	hah mee *koh*·muh

Making conversation

What do you like doing?	
Dé as toil leat/leibh a bhith a' dèanamh? (inf/pol)	jehs tawl laht/laiv uh vee uh *dee*·uh·nuhv
Do you like...?	
An toil leat/leibh...? (inf/pol)	uhn tawl laht/laiv...
Do you like sport?	
An toil leat/leibh spòrs? (inf/pol)	uhn tawl laht/laiv sporsh
Do you like drama?	
An toil leat/leibh dràma? (inf/pol)	uhn tawl laht/laiv *drah*·muh?
What kind of music do you like?	
Dè an seòrsa ciùil as toil leat/leibh? (inf/pol)	jen *shawr*·suh *kyoo*·il uhs tawl laht/laiv
Do you have any children?	
A' bheil clann agad/agaibh? (inf/pol)	uh vel klown *ah*·kuht/*ah*·kif
I like...	
Is toil leam...	stawl luhm...
I don't like...	
Cha toil leam...	hah tawl luhm...
I'd like...	
Bu toil leam...	buh tawl luhm...
I wouldn't like...	
Cha bu toil leam...	hah buh tawl luhm...

“THA MI DUILICH

– I'M SORRY”

Would you like...?	
Am bu toil leat/ leibh...? (inf/pol)	uhm buh tawl laht/ laiv...
Yes, I'd like that	
Bu toil	buh tawl
No, I wouldn't like that	
Cha bu toil	hah buh tawl

Going out

What are you doing this evening?	
Dè tha thu/sibh a' dèanamh feasgar? (inf/pol)	jeh hah oo/shif uh *jee*·uh·nuhv *fesk*·uhr
Would you like to go for a drink?	
Am bu toil leat/leibh a dhol a ghabhail dràm? (inf/pol)	uhm buh tawl laht/laiv uh ghawl uh *gah*·vuhl drahm
Would you like to go for a meal?	
Am bu toil leat/leibh a dhol gu biadh? (inf/pol)	uhm buh tawl laht/laiv uh ghawl guh *bee*·ughh
That'd be great	
Bhiodh sin sgoinneil	*vee*·ugh shin *skawn*·yuhl
I'm sorry, I can't	
Tha mi duilich, chan urrainn dhomh	hah mee *doo*·likh khahn *oo*·rin ghawm

FESTIVAL TIME

The annual Gaelic arts festival, usually held in early October at different locations around Scotland, is known as *am Mòd* (pronounced 'uhm mawt'). It's a competition-based festival which celebrates the Gaelic language and culture through music, dance, drama, arts and literature. The Mòd attracts visitors and competitors from across the globe.

WELL-WISHING

Happy birthday!
Co-là breith sona dhut! koh·lah breh *soh*·nuh ghoot

Happy Christmas!
Nollaig Chridheil! *naw*·lik *khree*·uhl

Happy New Year!
Bliadhna Mhath Ùr! *blee*·uh·nuh vah oor

Congratulations!
Meal do/ur naidheachd! (inf/pol) myahl doh/oor *neh*·yahkhk

Good luck.
Gun téid leat/leibh (inf/pol) goon chehj laht/laiv

Food

breakfast	**bracaist** (f)	*brah*·kishch
lunch	**lòn** (m)	lohn
dinner	**dìnnear** (f)	*jee*·nyuhr
drink	**deoch** (f)	jokh
food	**biadh** (m)	*bee*·uhgh
restaurant	**taigh-bidhe/ biadhlann** (m/f)	tai·*bee*·uh/ *bee*·uh·luhn

What would you like?
Dè tha thu ag iarraidh? jeh hah oo uhk *ee*·uh·ree

Give me..., please
Thoir dhomh... mas e do thoil e hawr ghawm... mahsh eh duh hawl eh

I'd like...
Tha mi ag iarraidh... hah mee uhk *ee*·uh·ree...

Are you hungry?	
A' bheil an t-acras ort?	uh vel uhn *tak*·ruhs awrsht
Are you thirsty?	
A' bheil am pathadh ort?	uh vel uhm *pah*·huhgh orsht
I'm hungry	
Tha an t-acras orm	hah uhn *tak*·ruhs *aw*·ruhm
I'm thirsty	
Tha am pathadh orm	hah uhn *pah*·huhgh *aw*·ruhm
I enjoyed that	
Chòrd sin rium	hawrsht shin ryoom
That was tasty	
Bha sin blasta	vah shin *blah*·stuh
That was really tasty	
Bha sin deagh bhlasta	vah shin joh *vlah*·stuh
I'd like some more	
Tha mi ag iarraidh tuilleadh	hah mee uhk *ee*·uh·ree *too*·lyuhgh

In the pub

I'd like a...	**Bu toil leam...**	buh tawl luhm...
glass of red wine	**glainne fìon dearg**	*glah*·nyuh *fee*·uhn je·ruhk
glass of whisky	**glainne uisge-beatha**	*glah*·nyuh *oosh*·kuh·*beh*·huh
glass of white wine	**glainne fìon geal**	*glah*·nyuh *fee*·uhn gyahl
half-pint of beer	**leth-phinnt leann**	*leh*·feench lyown
pint of beer	**pinnt leann**	peench lyown

"UISGE-BEATHA
– WHISKY"

It's my round	
'Se an turas agamsa a tha ann	sheh uhn *too*·ruhs *ah*·kuhm·suh hown
I'll get this one (man speaking)	
Gheobh mise am fear seo	yoh *mee*·shuh uhm fehr shaw
I'll get this one (woman speaking)	
Gheobh mise an tè seo	yoh *mee*·shuh uhn cheh shaw
What will you have?	
Dè ghabhas tu/sibh? (inf/pol)	jeh *gah*·vuhs too/shif
The same again	
An aon rud a-rithist	uhn ern root uh *ree*·ishch
I've had enough, thanks	
Tha gu leòr agam, tapadh leat/leibh (inf/pol)	ha guh lyawr *ah*·kuhm *tah*·puh laht/laiv
Cheers!	
Slàinte mhòr!	*slahn*·chuh vohr

Cornish

Cornish is a Celtic language related to Welsh and Breton. It ceased to function as a community language in the 18th century but was revived early in the 20th century. However, there are only 300-odd fluent Cornish speakers in Cornwall.

Key sounds in Cornish include *dh* (pronounced liked the *th* in 'this' or 'that') and *kh* (pronounced like *ch* in 'loch').

1	**unn**	een
2	**dew/diw** (m/f)	dew/deew
3	**tri/teyr** (m/f)	tree/tair
4	**peswar/peder** (m/f)	*pez*·wahr/*pe*·der
5	**pymp**	pimp
6	**hwegh**	whaykh
7	**seyth**	saith
8	**eth**	ehth
9	**naw**	now
10	**deg**	daig

Good morning
Myttin da *mit*·teen da

Good day
Dydh da didh da

Good afternoon
Dohajydh da do·*ha*·jidh da

Good evening
Gorthugher da gawth·*ee*·her da

How are you?
Fatla genes? *fat*·la *gen*·nes

" DYDH DA
— GOOD DAY "

Very well, (thank you)
Yn poynt da, (meur rasta) in poynt da (mur *ras*·ta)

And you?
Ha ty? ha tee

Good night!
Nos dha! nawz dha

Goodbye (to one person)
Dyw genes dew *gen*·nes

Goodbye (to more than one person)
Dyw genowgh dew *gen*·nohkh

Can you speak Cornish?
A wodhesta kewsel Kernewek? a *wo*·dhes·ta *kew*·zel kur·*new*·ek

Yes, I speak a little
Gonn, y kewsav boghes gon a *kew*·zaf *bow*·khez

No, I can't speak Cornish very well
Na wonn, ny gowsav Kernewek yn ta nah won nee *go*·zaf kur·*new*·ek in ta

Do you understand?
A wodhesta konvedhes? a *wo*·dhes·ta kon·*ve*·dhez

Yes, I understand
Gonn, my a gonvedh gon mee a *gon*·vedh

No, I don't understand
Na wonn, ny gonvedhav nah won nee gon·*ve*·dhaf

Scots (Lallans)

Lallans is spelt the way it's pronounced, so there are no separate pronunciation guides in this section.

1	**ae/ane**
2	**twa**
3	**three**
4	**fower**
5	**five**
6	**sax**
7	**sieven**
8	**aicht**
9	**nine**
10	**ten**

"FARE YE WEEL
— GOODBYE"

Good morning	**Guid mornin**
Good day	**Guid day**
Good afternoon	**Guid efter nune**
Good evening	**Guid e'en**
Good night	**Guid nicht**
Goodbye	**Fare ye weel**
How are you?	**Hou's aw wi ye?**
Fine, thank you	**Guid, thank ye**

I can't complain	**A canna compleen**
And you?	**And yersel?**
Come back soon	**Haste ye back**
Can you speak Lallans?	**Can ye speak Lallans?**
Yes, I speak a little	**Aye, a wee bit**
No, I can't speak Lallans very well	**No, ah canna speak Lallans very weel**
Do you understand?	**Dae ye unnerstaun?**
Yes, I understand	**Aye, ah unnerstaun**

Notes

Wordfinder

B

WORDFINDER

C

D

E

WORDFINDER

F

G

H

I

WORDFINDER

M

N

O

P

Q

R

S

WORDFINDER

T

Y

Z

Index

I

J

L

M

N

O

P

Q

R

S

T

V

W

Look out for these...

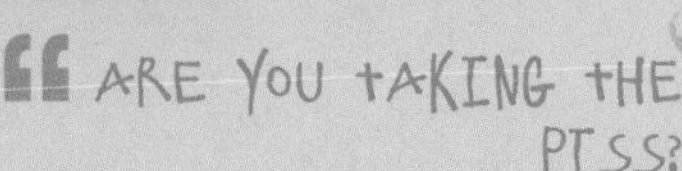

"ARE YOU TAKING THE PISS?
— ARE YOU MOCKING ME?"

"CHUFFED TO BITS
— DELIGHTED; PLEASED"

"THE DOG'S BOLLOCKS
— GREAT; TOP-QUALITY; SUCCESSFUL OR THE BEST"

"NAFF
— TACKY, UNFASHIONABLE OR UNCOOL"

"TROLLEYED
— DRUNK"